GREAT AND SMALL THINGS

From a Photograph of the Young Gorilla, "John" (1920).

Frontispiece]

GREAT AND SMALL THINGS

BY

Sir EDWIN RAY LANKESTER

WITH THIRTY-EIGHT ILLUSTRATIONS

Essay Index Reprint Series

 BOOKS FOR LIBRARIES PRESS
FREEPORT, NEW YORK

First Published 1923
Reprinted 1972

Library of Congress Cataloging in Publication Data

Lankester, Sir Edwin Ray, 1847-1929.
   Great and small things.

   (Essay index reprint series)
   Reprint of the 1923 ed.
   1. Zoology--Addresses, essays, lectures.
2. Science--Addresses, essays, lectures. I. Title.
QL81.L35 1972   591'.08   72-5630
ISBN 0-8369-2995-0

PRINTED IN THE UNITED STATES OF AMERICA

PREFACE

THE title of this little book is, I venture to say, appropriate to a miscellaneous collection of short papers in which subjects of widely differing interest are briefly brought to the reader's attention. They all relate to the study of living things ranging from the phagocyte to the gorilla, from the pond-snail to the Russian giant, from facts about longevity to theories as to human progress and the cruelty of Nature. Most of the chapters were written originally for publication in daily and weekly journals and have been now to some extent re-written and illustrated by text figures for the present volume.

E. RAY LANKESTER

December 1922

CONTENTS

LIST OF ILLUSTRATIONS

GREAT AND SMALL THINGS

CHAPTER I

THE GORILLA OF SLOANE STREET

AS the frontispiece to this volume, and as a text-figure (Fig. 1) in the present chapter, we have reproductions of two photographic portraits of a young gorilla. They are taken from a young male, probably a little less than five years old, which was brought by a French officer from the Gaboon and was purchased from him by the well-known dealer, Mr. Hamlyn, in July 1918. The gorilla was acquired by another owner (Major Penny) in December of that year, and was taken charge of by a lady (Miss Cunningham) who carried on a milliner's business in Sloane Street. I am indebted to her for my personal acquaintance with " John " and for many details as to his tastes and habits. She was remarkably successful in the management of this most interesting lodger. " John," as he was called, was thoroughly healthy and happy, and presented a great contrast to the sickly-looking anthropoids which are kept in cages in stuffy, overheated rooms in most zoological gardens. John enjoyed—in fact, owed his healthy condition to—fresh air and human society. He was taught to be perfectly clean, and had no taint of the monkey-house about him. He was fairly obedient, though requiring " an eye on him " to keep him out of mischief. He had his own room and bed, a garden to play in, a tree to climb (an exercise in which he did not excel), and he took his meals regularly in company.

Fig. 1.—Profile of the young Gorilla " John."

He was never left to mope alone, and was only separated from human companionship at night when he went to bed. He was very affectionate, good-natured, and intelligent, with, of course, preferences and aversions and some curious " terrors." A certain child's gollywog was for long a bogy to him, and was used as such to keep him from wandering. He passed through the winter oı 1918–19 in perfect health, the ordinary temperature of a dwelling-house being apparently quite warm enough for him. In the summer he went up with an attendant in a motor-car regularly, on three days of the week, to the Zoological Gardens in Regent's Park, and was on view in one of the open cages kindly placed at his disposal by the lions. He was, however, miserable while there, and eagerly awaited his return journey to Sloane Street.

He was very exclusive and dainty about food— perhaps owing to the fact that he had not been long trained by the example of his parents and relatives before he left the Gaboon. He ate all kinds of fruit (oranges, bananas, apples, raspberries, etc.), and took milk readily —also the white of a boiled egg, but rejected the yolk. He was dubious about roots (carrots, potatoes, turnips), and showed no taste for meat, though he would eat a little boiled fish. He rejected farinaceous food, but sweets—especially jam—were very welcome to him. He ate flowers—I have seen him help himself to and eat a dozen roses, one after the other—being attracted by their scent. A weakness for perfume led him to eat scented soap ; but in this he was not encouraged. Butter and pea-nut butter, dried dates, figs, raisins, prunes, Virol, and jellies of all sorts he loved. He took very little bread, whilst—contrary to what one would expect—nuts of any kind gave him terrible indigestion and pain. He soon got tired of any one food, and the lady who managed him believed that the secret of success with him was great variation in diet. He was very fond of tea and coffee. When it was cold he slept with a blanket over him, as his room was not specially heated. When sleeping, he lay on his back with arms and legs folded, but often on his side with his hand under his head. He would smile (some would say " grin "), giggle when tickled, and also roll on the floor and cry like a spoiled child when one refused to take him on to one's knee. He made other sounds, difficult to describe, signifying satisfaction, surprise, fright, and anger. Like a child, he was very fond of " showing off," and would repeatedly climb on to a table in order to take full-length dives into a spring-stuffed sofa close at hand, and then turn head over heels, laugh, and clap his hands. He was a restless little fellow and never tired of taking one by the hand and making one walk by his side until he brought one to the window, which he would unfasten and open, or to the door, upon which he would beat a tattoo, or to some piece of furniture, or to the staircase, where he would eagerly display his gymnastic capacities.

But the most interesting thing he would do when excited and " showing off " was to stand up and beat his chest alternately with right and left hand at the rate of about four blows to the second. I was greatly astonished and pleased when he behaved thus on my first visit to him in Sloane Street. I believe that no one has testified to this behaviour on the part of a gorilla since Paul Du Chaillu described it. I knew that much-maligned little man, Paul Du Chaillu, very well. He was a genuine naturalist and observer, and brought many new things to London from the Gaboon (where he had business connections) besides the skins and skulls of gorillas and chimpanzees (*e.g.* the great water insecti-vore Potamogale). Later he wrote an interesting book on Norway and early Norse art. But he did not know the English language when he first came to London, and

he entrusted his notes and diary of travels to an American
assistant who made a hash of them—confusing dates and
itineraries.   Du Chaillu's genuine experiences were so
novel and entertaining that when inconsistencies were
discovered in his dates and the details of his journeys,
he was assailed by malicious critics as a second Munc-
hausen. Special discredit and ridicule were given to
his account of the male gorilla beating his breast in
defiance and advancing to attack the adventurous hunter.
Huxley—whose account of the anthropoid apes in his
book " Man's Place in Nature " is still the best we have
—is careful to state that he sees no reason to disbelieve
Du Chaillu's account of the habits of the gorilla, and in
especial of this " breast-beating " habit. It is an interesting fact that the gorilla's close relative, the chimpanzee, has never been seen to beat its breast, and that
the young gorilla John exhibited this proof of his
paternity as soon as he got a little bit " puffed up " by
admiring attention.

John's height when standing in a normal position
(that is to say, bending forward a little) was, in January
1920, 2 inches less than 3 feet. He measured from hip
to head 21 inches, and from hip to heel 17 inches. He
grew considerably during the year 1919, but no records
were kept of his height nor of his weight. His face was
absolutely black, with the exception of the lips. The
surface of this black skin was bright and polished, reflecting the light. The fur was a dark brown. By his
jet-black face he differed from the chimpanzee of Sierra
Leone, which has a pale muzzle, and from the more
or less pinky-brown-faced varieties of chimpanzee from
the Gaboon. The bald chimpanzee called " Nschiego-
mbouvé " (its local name) by Du Chaillu has a black
face, and is perhaps entitled to recognition as a sub-

species or variety of chimpanzee under the name
" calvus."   " Sally," the chimpanzee who lived for six
years at the Gardens in Regent's Park, and was constantly visited and studied by me, was one of this race,
and, in spite of her black face, differed greatly in
physiognomy and character, as well as in " size-
for-age," from the gorilla John.

Our photographs of John show two characteristic
features in which the gorilla differs from the chimpanzee
—namely, the relatively much smaller size of the ear
and the prominence of the large expanded nostrils, a
feature not properly seen in " stuffed " specimens.   The
attitude of John when walking was practically the
same as that of the chimpanzee, the body being supported on the knuckles of the flexed hands (contrary to
the original statements of Dr. Savage), whilst the feet
were turned with the soles inward, the weight resting
on the outer margin of the foot and heel, the great toe
and the smaller toes being turned inwards, slightly
flexed and not applied to the ground.   It is, however,
the fact that John not unfrequently stood and sometimes
walked with the sole and heel applied as a flat surface to
the ground—the " plantar " face of the toes also being
applied to the supporting surface—the great toe extending inwards, its axis forming, on the horizontal plane,
a right angle with that of the diverging group of smaller
toes.   Mr. Pocock informs me that chimpanzees also
sometimes walk or stand with the foot and toes thus
applied to the ground, and he has seen them when
sitting down, swing their feet alternately and beat the
floor of their cage with the flat of the foot, for the purpose
of making a rhythmical " noise."

The hallux, or great toe of man, is derived from an

ancestor with a large hallux, which has been transmitted equally to man and to the anthropoid apes. But
in man the foot has become so modified that the mechanical axis of the hind-limb is continued through the
hallux, which in turn is directed forward (instead of to
the inner face of the limb) so as to effect this result. The
great ridge-line of the shin bone's edge is continued, without divergence from its straight course, by the tendons of
the hallux at the instep to the end of that toe in an un-
distorted human foot (Fig. 4). Man's foot is not planti-
grade like that of the baboons and bears, in which the
axial line of the limb passes between the third and
fourth digits. Nor does it show any trace of having
ever been capable of " grasping " by the thumb-like
movement of the hallux across the plantar surface as in
apes. It is hallucigrade or halluci-axial—the smaller
ineffective group of toes being thrown by the special
development of the human hind-limb away from the
axial line of the limb and hallux to its outer side—as
one may see by looking at one's own naked foot pointed
forward as in the act of stepping (Figs. 2, 3, and 4).
The difference in the form and mechanism of the foot of
man and of the man-like apes is more profound than is
any other structural difference which separates them.
We have no knowledge of any intermediate condition of
the foot—no trace of any connecting link nor of the
history of the development of the human foot.[1]

[1] An entirely erroneous figure of the gorilla's foot is given by Mr.
Akeley in an interesting article in " The World's Work " of October
1922. He gives valuable observations on the habits of the gorilla
made when hunting this animal in the neighbourhood of Lake Kivu,
in Central Africa. He made casts of the head, hands, and feet of
specimens killed by him. But the cast of the foot is (as shown in
a photograph) strangely distorted and made to present a false resemblance to the foot of man. Since Mr. Akeley was securing specimens of gorilla for the American Museum in New York, it is well that
his mistake about the gorilla's foot should be corrected at once.

A careful and detailed anatomical comparison of the foot of man and that of the man-like apes should, it seems probable, enable a morphologist of imagination to determine what has been the most probable ancestral history of both, and what was the structure and mechanical adaptation of the foot of their common

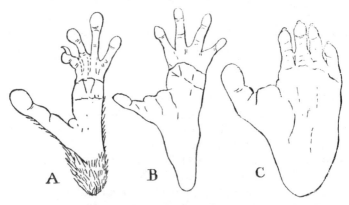

FIG. 2.—Views of the plantar surface of the foot, A, of a Lemur (Propithecus diadema—a species which habitually walks on its hind-legs) ; B, of an Old-World Monkey (Cercopithecus) ; C, of a Gorilla, represented as of approximately the same length. They are intended to show the proportionate size of the great toe (very large) and of the other toes in each kind, and also to show the natural position of the great toe when the animal is standing on the flat or "plantar" surface of the foot. Note the wide gap between the great toe and the second toe. (Reproduced by permission from drawings published by Mr. Pocock, F.R.S.)

ancestor. No such attempt to imagine the ancestral modifications of the human foot has yet been made with adequate employment of existing data. Such facts as the correlation of variation of the fore- and the hind-limb, and therefore the history of the thumb as well as of the great toe, would have to be considered. The history of the modification of the fore- and hind-foot in other groups, besides that of the Primates, must be searched for suggestions as to their history in man and the anthro-

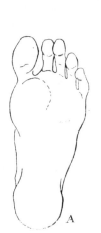

FIG. 3.

A, view of the plantar surface of a human foot—to compare with Fig. 2. The great toe is much larger proportionately to the other toes than in the gorilla ; the gap between the great toe and second toe is very greatly lessened, and the great toe is not directed away from the mechanical axis of the foot, but is traversed by it.

B is a reproduction of the " tread " or " print " of a human foot, obtained by inking the plantar surface and then letting the foot tread on a flat sheet of paper.

FIG. 4.—Outline drawing of the upper face of the human foot and its relation to the leg, showing the continuation of the shin-ridge or tibial axis by the great toe.

poids. Form and proportions of the digits and of the tarsal bones, as puzzling as those of man and possibly capable of throwing light on the history of the human foot, are shown by the great extinct Australian Marsupial Diprotodon exhibited in the Natural History Museum. This animal had a huge massive heel-bone and very small digits, resembling those of man. (See my " Extinct Animals," fig. 135.) Man's conception of the ground plan and mechanism of his own foot has varied at different times and in different races—as is shown by the differing and often injurious forms of " foot-wear," the " sandals," boots and shoes of past and present times. The " sandal " does not distort the natural disposition of the toes : the large gap between the great toe and the second toe is maintained, and a fastening strap passes through it. But the leather shoe and the wooden sabot both ignore the true and natural pose of the great toe and squeeze all the toes together, so as to give a false " point " to the distorted foot in the line of the second toe—an artificial axis.

The question as to whether there is one or more species of gorilla is in a state similar to that as to the species of chimpanzees. It is stated that specimens from different localities differ in the colour of the hair and its abundance, and also in size and in the development of the bony crests in the skull of the male. But we have not a sufficient number of specimens nor such detailed information with regard to these varieties as to warrant any conclusion as to the existence even of well-marked local varieties. On the other hand, such local varieties or sub-species are very common among the larger African mammalia, and may occur among gorillas. There is no doubt that the hair of the gorilla becomes lighter and decidedly grey with age.

As to the size attained by the gorilla, exaggerated estimates have been given by measuring from the top (crown) of the head to the tip of the toes of the stretched foot (which is of great length), instead of to the heel. The adult male measured from the heel is from about 5 ft. 2 in. to nearly 6 ft. in exceptional cases, but in the natural position with knuckles on the ground the animal would stand from 4 ft. to 4½ ft. high. A specimen measuring 5 ft. 5 in. from the heel to the crown weighed 500 lb. (35 st. 10 lb.)—a fact which gives an indication of its heavy, unwieldy figure, the body being relatively to the legs much larger than in man. The average height of females (heel to crown) is 4 ft. 6 in.

Gorillas have been brought from time to time to the Zoological Society's Gardens, but have not lived long. The following is a list of such specimens kindly given me by Mr. Pocock : *Male*, purchased October 1887 ; lived two months. *Female*, purchased March 1896 ; lived five months. *Female* (baby), purchased August 1904 ; lived three weeks. *Female* (about six years old), purchased August 1904 ; lived five weeks. *Female*, deposited August 1905 ; sent to America after ten days. *Female* (baby), deposited in March 1906 ; lived barely two months. *Male* (baby), deposited in March 1908 ; lived one week.

Recently the Zoological Society of Dublin had a young specimen which lived for three years in the Society's menagerie. It is difficult to discover records of gorillas in continental menageries, or of any which may have been in the hands of showmen. A female is, however, stated to have lived for seven years in Breslau, and it would be interesting to have any trustworthy notes about that specimen. At the Berlin Gardens one was kept for about twelve months. Hagenbeck, the dealer and owner of the celebrated Gardens near Berlin, spent

£600 on gorillas in one season, and then, as he told
Mr. Pocock, dropped them as a hopeless investment,
because they die so quickly! The one case of the
female at Breslau shows that there may be individual
qualities or methods of management—of which I should
be glad to hear—which favour the survival of the gorilla
when brought to Northern Europe.

It is of some interest to note that the name " gorilla "
was given to this animal in 1847 by Dr. Savage, a
missionary who lived for many years in the Gaboon and
gave a very full description of the animal. The word
" gorilla " is applied in an extant ancient Greek work
giving an account of the voyage of Hanno the Cartha-
ginian in the fifth or sixth century B.C., to certain hairy
savage people discovered by him in an island on the
African coast. Dr. Savage used this name for the
larger of the two apes of the Gaboon without committing
himself to the suggestion that this ape was the creature
seen by Hanno, and at that date so-called by the more
affable natives. It is indeed the general opinion, at
present, that Hanno's " gorillas " were baboons—the
word " drill " now used for them (e.g. mandrill) being
possibly related to the earlier term " go-rilla." The
present native name in the Gaboon for the gorilla is
enjé-ena, whilst enjé-eko is the name of the smaller of the
two apes—the chimpanzee. At an earlier date (1625)
we learn from " Purchas his Pilgrimes," in the relation
of the strange adventures of one Andrew Battell, who
for eighteen years was a prisoner of the Portuguese in
Angola, that " the woods are covered with baboons,
monkeys, apes, and parrots," and " that here also are
two kinds of monsters which are common in these woods
and very dangerous. The greatest of these two monsters
is called Pongo in their language and the lesser is called

Engeco." Battell then proceeds to give a vivid description of the " pongo," which leaves no doubt that it is the gorilla of our nomenclature—the enjé-ena of the modern natives—to which he refers as the pongo, whilst the smaller " monster " is the chimpanzee, still known to the natives by the name " enjeco," which, according to Buffon, has been corrupted by Europeans into " enjocko " and " jocko."

The confusion of the two African apes with the Oriental orang-utan, and the embarrassing interchange both of their native and scientific appellations by learned zoologists of the past, form a story which may be read in Huxley's " Man's Place in Nature." I am only concerned here to say a brief word about the scientific names applied to the gorilla and his smaller associate, the chimpanzee. There is some disagreement in the zoological world as to the " correct " name to be used for these animals when scientific accuracy is desired. The actual decision in these matters is dependent on priority, and so eventually on history. But I will merely say that it seems to me inconvenient to place the gorilla and the chimpanzee (that is, the enjé-enas and the enjé-ekos) in one genus, Troglodytes. I prefer the practice of those who call the bigger ape Gorilla savagei (after its first careful describer), and leave the chimpanzee alone in the genus Troglodytes. But the latter is usually called by the specific name " niger," which seems to be open to correction (according to strict rules), because he is remarkable for being (as a rule) *not* black but pale-faced. I should therefore wish to call him Troglodytes enjecko. It would no doubt be convenient to use the specific name " enjena " for the gorilla, and so respect the native authorities who long ago distinguished the two great African apes as " en-jena " and " en-jecko." It is desirable to enumerate, and for that purpose to name each of the observed varieties respectively of Gorilla savagei and of Troglodytes enjecko, but to call each of those varieties a distinct species is not consistent with the practice of zoologists in regard to other groups of animals.

I regret to have to state that, owing to the expense involved in keeping John in a private house and the natural anxiety as to whether he could be kept at all in such conditions when he reached maturity, his owner was induced to sell him, in the belief that he was to be specially cared for in a warm climate. He was taken by his new proprietor to the United States, and became very ill owing to his separation from the friend who had hitherto cared for him and loved him. The temporary separation of a few hours, when (in the summer of 1920) he used to be taken to the Zoological Gardens in London, had always caused him great distress. This novel and complete exile utterly prostrated him ; it deprived him of all spirit and appetite. An atack of pneumonia killed him soon after his arrival in America. I agree with those who hold that a grave responsibility is undertaken when the attempt is made to bring up a wild animal in a cage or even in the enclosed paddocks of a secluded park. Fortunately there are many animals which can be easily brought up in captivity in complete health and happiness. But there are others which require very special conditions. Among these latter are the man-like apes, which require companionship and friendship in order to thrive. The gorilla is the most sensitive among them, and at the same time the most difficult to deal with, on account of the great size and strength to which it attains after a few years of growth, and the probability of its developing hostility to its human associates and consequent " ferocity " after the age of puberty. It must be a terrible thing to have to destroy a trustful, happy animal, such as was John the young gorilla, when it approaches full growth and maturity. Yet it seems that there are only two other courses which can be pursued by those who, not being millionaires, have removed such animals from their native forests and successfully nurtured them during their youth—namely (1) the animals may be returned to their original surroundings and set at liberty before reaching full growth, or else (2) kept in iron-barred cages as prisoners. In the former case they would probably die from want of habituation to those original conditions, unable to find food or to cope with their wild relatives ; in the latter case they would pine and die after a more or less prolonged endurance of the misery resulting from loss of companionship and liberty. I confess that it seems to me that no one should " adopt " a young gorilla who is not possessed of a large income and able to pay for skilled attendants and courageous companions for him when he is " grown up." Perhaps there would be a chance of success if a happy pair could be provided for—within an enclosed park in a tropical or sub-tropical climate ! That would be a very costly experiment, but it is the only one which offers the chance of healthy life to a captive gorilla.

[Miss Alyse Cunningham, who tended and taught John for two years, has published in the "Bulletin of the Zoological Society of New York," September 1921, a full account of him, illustrated by several excellent photographs, of which the most attractive shows John seated by his playmate—a little girl three years old.]

CHAPTER II

SCIENCE AND THE FILM

I T is only equitable that the great industry of cinema-
film production should give valuable help to the
investigation of nature—since it owes its own
existence to the persevering inquiries of scientific men
seeking to ascertain exactly the movements of the legs
of the horse when engaged in that rapid action which is
called the " gallop."

About forty years ago, photography was advanced
to a new position of power by two discoveries—that of
the dry plate or film and that of the means of rendering
instantaneous exposure effective in place of the long
exposure previously necessary. Not only was the
venerable science of astronomy rejuvenated by these
discoveries, which enabled the astronomer to print the
photographic records of hundreds of thousands of stars
invisible to the human eye, even when fortified by the
most powerful telescopes, but the study of movement of
all kinds—from that of the waves of the sea, to that of
the limbs of the swiftest animals, including the most
fleeting expressions of the human face and the flickering
of the " cilia " of the minutest animalcules scarcely
visible with the highest powers of the microscope—
entered upon a totally new path. It became not only
possible but easy to obtain by instantaneous photo-

graphy, a series of successive permanent pictures of a quickly changing scene at the rate of twenty or more in the second, showing what the eye is not quick enough to distinguish—namely, the detailed phases and succession of the movements which follow one another so rapidly as to elude our attempts to see more than their general result. In the special case studied, namely, the galloping horse, a blurred eye-picture of moving parts, now here, now there, defying our efforts to disentangle the order and significance of their movement, was resolved by the series of instantaneous photographs into sharply cut definite shapes following one another with perfect regularity and order and comprehensible as the successive phases of the continued movement thus analysed.

The " problem of the galloping horse," which had long engaged the attention of artists, sportsmen, and experimentalists, was thus solved by the American photographer, Muybridge. It had been maintained that in the " gallop " the horse never has all four feet off the ground : others held that the " flying gallop," with fore- and hind-limbs fully stretched and all the feet free from contact with the ground, as depicted in Herring's well-known " racing plates " of last century, was a correct representation of one phase of the movement of the legs of the galloping horse. Large wagers were actually offered and taken as to the facts in dispute. I have discussed this matter at length elsewhere (" Science from an Easy Chair," Second Series, 1912), and will here merely recall the fact that by using carefully contrived apparatus—consisting of a row of cameras placed at intervals along a running track, the shutters of which were opened and closed electrically by the passage of the horse in front of them—Muybridge succeeded in

2

obtaining a series of accurately timed photographic pictures of the galloping horse, each taken by about 1–40th of a second's exposure and separated from its predecessor and from its successor by an equally short interval. The true series of movements made by the horse's legs in the action, or " gait," known as " the gallop," were thus accurately recorded. It was shown that the legs never assume simultaneously the position represented in " the flying gallop "—nor any position resembling it — although all four legs do simultaneously leave the ground for the fraction of a second and are curiously flexed beneath the animal's body.

And then came the moment in history when this photographic investigation of animal movement gave birth to the vast industry known as the " cinematograph," " biograph," or " movies." When lecturing in London and showing his series of instantaneous photographs of the horse (and of other animals, including man), Muybridge (whom I often met at the time) was led to make the experiment (first tried at the Royal Institution in Albemarle Street) of viewing his photographs by the then well-known device called the " Zoetrope," or " Wheel of Life." The " Zoetrope " is a hollow cylinder a foot and a half in diameter, turning on a vertical axis rapidly and having its surface pierced with a number of vertical slots. Round the interior is arranged a paper band of pictures representing successive phases of a figure in movement, such as a dancer or a juggler or a running animal. When the cylinder is rotated an observer looking through the slots sees the figure apparently in motion. The figures were printed or painted in black " silhouette " on the paper bands supplied with the " Zoetrope " by dealers. Muybridge substituted for these hand-painted figures his series of instantaneous photographs of the galloping horse The detached, queer and awkward-looking, but faithful, *instantanées* gave, when looked at through the slot as the cylinder revolved at the appropriate rate, a single moving picture of the galloping horse, formed by the fusion in the observer's visual apparatus of the rapidly passing photographs. It was easy to throw the pictures on the screen by a slight modification of the " Zoetrope " and the use of the electric lantern, and thus the first " cinema show " was created.

The subsequent development of the modern " cinema " was brought about by the invention of the celluloid roll-film, on which a series of many thousands of consecutive pictures are impressed by instantaneou photography, the sensitized film being moved across the focal plane and exposed intermittently. The film is developed and printed off in a permanent condition on similar celluloid films, which are then put through the exhibition camera for projection, with vast enlargement, on a distant screen. They are " jerked " through it with the same intermittence, and at the same rate as that at which the photographs were taken ; or, if desired, more quickly or more slowly.

Permanent Records.—The cinema appeals to the scientific investigator because it offers to him two distinct and widely separate new means of gaining knowledge. The first is that of obtaining *records* of the movements of all sorts of animate and inanimate things as they affect our vision—permanent pictures of " the fleeting scene," showing things actually moving and changing in shape and position as we see them with our eyes and as we could only, until the cinema came to our aid, recall or memorize by lengthy and necessarily inadequate words or by series of hand-made drawings. Many "cinema" records which are of value to science have already been made, and many more are yet to be made.

Among these are those of the dances and other movements of remote races of mankind, such as are practised by the natives of Central Australia, recorded in cinema films, and shown to us here in London by Sir Baldwin Spencer, F.R.S., a few years ago (1914). In Sir Baldwin's exhibition, the realization of an extremely remote and inaccessible phase of humanity, was greatly aided by the use of the phonograph, which gave to us the rhythmical chant or song of the "black fellows," taken simultaneously with the film pictures of their ceremonial dancing. A knowledge of the dances and ceremonials of primitive people is of very great importance to the science of anthropology, and unless such records are taken now we shall never get them : for the customs of primitive people die out and disappear even more rapidly than the people themselves. Again, in the same way the cinema can give us invaluable records of the habits and movements of wild animals destined soon to disappear and even now remote from us and difficult of access. To a very small extent such films have been taken, but there is need for more determined work of the kind, carried out systematically and thoroughly, with scientific purpose and professional skill Another wonderful series of movements which are but rarely open to our inspection are those of microscopic organisms. They can be filmed, and so "recorded," by the combination of microscope and cinema-camera. Those produced by Messrs. Pathé, of Paris, especially those of blood parasites, have a real value for science.

Slowing-down of Movement.—The other kind of service rendered by the cinema to science is in a way accidental or unintentional. The cinema show contains in fact " more than meets the eye of man." The desire to *analyse* the movements of the galloping horse led to the making of the moving pictures of the cinema show. And now the cinema films printed with thousands of instantaneous photographs in series—to be used merely to produce a moving picture—offer to the scientific inquirer the analysis of the various movements seen in the picture in a most convenient form. Each instantaneous photograph on the film furnishes the observer with an instantaneous phase of this or that movement. The movements are, in fact, analysed into their constituent phases, lasting each but 1–40th of a second or less. Although in practice these separate instantaneous pictures are so quickly passed through the projecting lantern as to be inseparable by the eye from one another, yet the film can be passed by jerks at longer intervals, or the film can be taken in the hand and each picture separately examined. Thus the ordinary walking and running of our fellow-citizens is shown to be built up of what are often very ugly instantaneous poses of the feet and legs, necessary results of our muscular and skeletal structure.

The expression of the emotions (on which Darwin wrote a book) is analysed in a surprising way by these constituent pictures of the film, and a field of valuable observation on that important subject is thus opened to the psychologist, which has not yet been surveyed. Examples are seen in the facial changes in Muybridge's series of the baseball batsman and in the series showing the face and movements of a naked bather suddenly drenched by a pailful of cold water.

The cinema shows have from time to time thrilled their spectators by the exhibition of films showing athletes boxing, jumping, running, and playing various games of ball, in which the passage of the film through the exhibition lantern is greatly " slowed down," but not enough to cause discontinuity of the moving figures. The " slowing," however, is such as to produce the most ludicrous appearance of hesitation and deliberate retarding of what is usually rapid instantaneous action. A boxer slowly and gently places his fist on the nose of his opponent, who quietly and ineffectually raises his arm in order gently to touch the intrusive fist. A high jumper is seen rising slowly in the air from the ground as though levitated by " spirits " or filled with gas, and then slowly, slowly, with astonishing contortions, he propels himself in a sitting position over the bar and quietly sinks, as though in a heavy liquid, to the ground once more. In the same way the deliberate, prolonged administration of a gentle push in the air to a tennis ball by a player who seems to be in a state of semi-somnolence is a wonderful and laughable result of slowing down the film of a first-class tennis match taken at a rapid rate. These slowed-down films—exhibited to the public for the sake of their grotesque suggestions—have great value as leading to the scientific analysis and understanding of complex movements, whether of limbs or of facial muscles, and render the separate, detached, instantaneous photographs readily intelligible. They also offer to the artist some very beautiful " poses " of the human body, as, for instance, in the slowed-down flight through the air of a " high " diver.

Movements of Legs and Wings.—Series of such *instantanées* must be made by the biologist expressly for his own inquiries, and every biological laboratory of university rank will soon have its own special apparatus (applicable to the microscope as well as to normal scenes) both for taking series of instantaneous pictures and for projecting them at whatever rate is desired on to a screen. A small apparatus of this kind suitable for use in an ordinary sitting-room or study is now on sale at a moderate price. I may give expression to personal conviction so far as to say that had such apparatus been available some thirty years ago, when I enjoyed the control of a laboratory and a staff of assistants and pupils at Oxford, I should certainly have had it installed there and have made researches by its aid. The movements of the legs and wings of all sorts of animals, large and small, besides those of the horse's legs, must be investigated in this way. The question which so much disquieted the centipede when addressed to her by the toad, according to a poem cited on p. 242 —namely, " Pray, which leg moves after which ? " must be answered. And this not only as to centipedes, but as to the even more elusive millipedes and the fascinating marine worms called Nereis and Eunice and Nephthys and Phyllodoce, which have a row of more than a hundred paddle-like legs on each side of the body, moving rhythmically and propelling the worm through the water whilst its body gracefully undulates like that of a serpent. That " rhythm " must be ascertained and its control by the nervous centres of the " annelid " (a prettier name than " worm ") explained.

Movements of Cilia.—Then, too, to name only one other line of inquiry in which the cinema can, and will at once, help biology, there is the investigation (long waiting for further progress) of the movements of the vibratile hairs called " cilia " and " flagella," by use of which a whole population of microscopic Infusoria—of hundreds of different kinds—move with agility and discrimination and also often create whirlpools sweeping food into their mouths. The movements of cilia are so rapid that they have caused divergence of opinions as to their character as great as those as to the galloping legs of the horse. More complex and calling more urgently for instantaneous photographic records are the movements of the single long flagella of such animalcules as Euglena, Astasia, and the so-called " monads." These " flagella " are sometimes, as in the spermatozoids of animals, worked as propulsive tails, like that of a tadpole, whilst another sort is carried as a straight stiff rod in front of the animalcule but has its free terminal portion bent back like the lash of a whip. This reflected lash wriggles in rhythmic undulation and so acts as a *traction-pull* and draws the animalcule forward. The exact movement of cilia and flagella and the action of various agencies in causing their variation could all be registered by series of instantaneous photographs taken by such a combination of the microscope and cinema camera as has enabled Dr. Commandant (who has pursued his excellent researches in the film factory of Messrs. Pathé, of Paris) to produce moving pictures of the minute bacteria and spirilla and of many animalcules with great accuracy and clearness of detail. Such an application of " cinema methods " to the needs of science will soon be realized.

Quickening Up.—Having mentioned the " slowing down " of films as a source of interesting information, I am reminded of the contrasted method of quickening

up a film which can give results of some value. For
instance, such a very slow gradual process as the opening of a flower-bud or leaf-bud, taking, say, three or
four days, can be photographed at intervals of several
minutes and a film of some hundreds of instantaneous
pictures thus obtained which is subsequently projected
at the rate of a thousand or more in a minute. The
resulting screen picture gives the untwisting of the flower
from bud to perfect expansion in about half a minute.
The whole process is visualized as one rapid movement, but not too rapid for the mind to form a
vivid impression of the form and character of the
movement.

The same thing has been shown in a much more
difficult field of study—namely, that of the self-division
and consequent multiplication of the constituent cells of
protoplasm which build up animal tissues. This process
is usually a very slow one. A cell, even in young tissue
which is rapidly growing, takes some six hours or more
to increase in bulk, and then to commence to split into
two by the division of its nucleus or central kernel. It
is so slow that it does not present itself to the observer's
mind as a movement at all. It is as difficult to " see "
as is the movement of the hour-hand of a watch. Yet
when a film is produced by photographing the dividing
cell of living tissue at intervals of half a minute, and
when the film so produced is unrolled at a much quicker
rate, so as to pass through in half a minute what took
six hours—then, indeed, we get a most astonishing
spectacle. The quiet little corpuscles or " cells " of
protoplasm suddenly become obviously " alive." They
were " alive " all the time, but their slow movement
failed to impress the observer. Now we see them in " the
quickened-up " film—swelling and pushing one another,

and then suddenly bursting or splitting into two, whereupon each half swells and proceeds on the same path of
growth and division

The quickening-up process helps us to put things
together, and to realize the active movement which is
going on, though too slowly to be obvious to us when not
thus accelerated.   It would in this way help us to understand the separate pictures on a film of a lawn-tennis
match, supposing we had only seen them very slowly
pass through an exhibition camera.   But as a means of
investigation, " quickening up " is not nearly so important as " slowing down," and the ultimate separation
of the constituent pictures of a film.   That is a process
of real analysis and promises to render valuable help
to scientific studies

Records of Great Actors and Dancers.—Before
leaving the subject, I should like to emphasize the
value of the service to all sorts of interests, arts, in-
dustries, and sciences, which the cinema can render
when used purely and simply to *register a record*—a
record, be it remembered, of a brief period of life and
movement.   This is altogether distinct from its use
as a source of amusement, as a teller of stories and a
peep-show of astonishing adventures, of horrors un-
speakable, and of beauties beyond words.   I confess
that I do not get so much pleasure from the cinema in
that sort of way as I do from the stage.   But it seems to
me that the cinema can fill a special place not possible
for the living drama and stage play.   It can actually
reproduce by its carefully executed faithful records,
the changing facial expression and the gestures of great
actors, of great public speakers, and of leaders of all
kinds of enterprise.   *It provides scientifically accurate*

records of evanescent phenomena. It has been little if at all used for this purpose, which appears to me to be its distinctive and indeed unique possibility—far more important than that of " story-telling without words." A few films have been produced which possess this special value. Such, for instance, is one of the first films shown in London in which the story of the murder of the Duc de Guise was " featured," as they say, by two great actors of the Comédie Française, M. Mounier Sully and M. Le Bargy, aided by other notable actors and actresses. The value of this film (which I saw when it was first exhibited) consists—if it still exists—not in the dramatic story which it tells, but in the permanent record of the methods and mastery of facial expression characteristic of a group of famous comedians.

There is one great art of the stage in which the cinema could preserve for us a really complete and entirely satisfactory presentation of the performance of specially gifted artists, which can be perpetuated in no other way. That is the creative art of the great dancer. So far as I know this record has never been attempted. Some ten years ago Mr. John Sargent, the Academician, said to me that no painter could possibly present on canvas the charm and artistic gifts of the great Russian dancer Madame Anna Pavlova. It could, he said, only be achieved by the cinematograph. No doubt this is true. It *could* be done by the cinema, but it never has been. I do not know what are the circumstances which have hitherto prevented the production of the most skilfully arranged films faithfully recording the performance of the greatest dancer of our time—films which would transmit to posterity with almost perfect accuracy the marvellous beauties of moving gesture and expression, which now are vouchsafed to us for a brief moment and remain thereafter only as fading memories. But some day the cinema will rescue the work of such great artists from oblivion and offer it for the permanent delight of the world.

CHAPTER III

THE PHAGOCYTES, OR EATER-CELLS

ALL living things, whether plants or animals, are either single very minute " corpuscles " of protoplasm—called " cells "—or are aggregates, *i.e.* built-up masses of such cells. Protoplasm is the name given to the very peculiar living, changing " slime " or viscid material of which every " cell " is constituted. The name " cell " was applied two hundred and fifty years ago to the tiny cases, fitted together like the cells of a honeycomb, which the living units, or corpuscles, of protoplasm building up the leaves, stems, flowers, and fruits of plants deposit around themselves. Then the application of the word was actually transferred from the cell or case to its living, slimy content—just as we say " a bottle of wine," meaning the liquid contained in the glass bottle and not the glass bottle itself.

Not only is every living thing built up by these units of living matter called " cells," and of the cases of inert material deposited by them around themselves, which may be either very copious or else negligible in quantity, but the fact is that every living thing, whether plant or animal, starts its individual existence as a single " fertilized egg-cell " usually less than 1–150th of an inch in diameter, which slowly increases in bulk and divides into two   Each of these two divides into two, and these repeat the process, and so on for hundreds of times, until from the single egg-cell—in the course of days or weeks —an adherent mass of many million " cells " may result. Such is the case with the larger animals and plants ; but there are simple kinds of both plants and animals which are *single cells* and remain so. They take nourishment, grow in size, and divide into two ; but the two, in this kind, separate from one another, and each goes on its own way. Such animals, of which many hundred kinds are known to microscopists, are called " unicellular animals " or " Protozoa." Each is comparable to a single one of the many million units which build up a large animal such as a man or a fish or a snail. And, similarly, there are unicellular plants.

Living cells acquire many different shapes and are variously active. It is not surprising that *some* amongst those building up a complex multicellular animal resemble very closely some of the independent unicellular animals. Whilst most of the cells of a multicellular animal are embedded in the case-like material which they form, and so constitute compact, more or less solid, living masses, which are called tissues, others float freely in the liquids of the animal body—the blood and the lymph—and are singularly like certain unicellular " animalcules " which are common in ponds and in sea-water, where they lead an independent life. These " animalcules " have long been known as Amœba or the Proteus-animalcule, and the floating cells similar to Amœbæ formed in the blood and lymph of multicellular animals by division of the original or parent " egg-cell," are called " white blood corpuscles," also " amœboid corpuscles," or, since Metchnikoff discovered their nature and importance, the " eater-cells," or " phagocytes."

Let us look first at an Amœba. In Fig. 5, one is shown removed from some pond-water and crawling on a glass slide. It is magnified about 200 times in diameter. The figures are actual photographs taken from the first cinema-film of a moving shape-changing Amœba ever produced, and were prepared and given to me by Messrs. Pathé, of Paris. The whole film

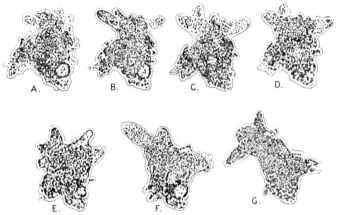

FIG. 5.—Figures from a cinema film of a rapidly moving Amœba photographed from life by Messrs. Pathé, of Paris. The complete series consists of photographs taken at the rate of thirty in a second of time. The figures here selected are about a second of time apart.

could not be printed here, but I have selected seven, showing the changes of shape of the Amœba at intervals of about one second of time. This constant change of shape is indicated by the name Amœba—which is a Greek word meaning " changeful." Owing to this irregular expansion and retraction of its naked slimy substance or " protoplasm," the Amœba crawls. But not only that. If it comes into the neighbourhood of a particle of food (a diatom or tiny plant-particle more minute than itself) the slimy substance of the Amœba is chemically attracted by it and flows around the food-particle and engulfs it, as shown in Fig. 6, A.   And the particle (*a*) so engulfed or swallowed by the Amœba

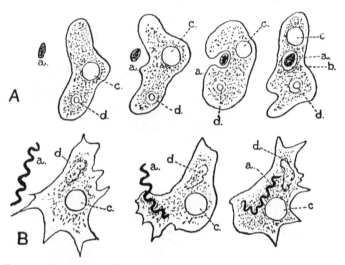

Fig. 6.—Comparison of an Amœba (A) and a Colourless Blood Corpuscle or Phagocyte (B).   Each is in the act of engulfing a food-particle.

The food-particle *a* in the case of the amœba is a minute green plant, and in the case of the phagocyte is a disease-germ of the kind known as a " spirillum " which produces " relapsing fever." The successive stages of the enclosure of the food-particle in the protoplasm or living substance of the amœba and the phagocyte are seen.   *a*, food-particle.   *b*, water taken in with it by the amœba.   *c*, vacuole or cavity in the protoplasm containing liquid. *d*, the " cell-nucleus " or central kernel.

with a little water (*b*) is digested and dissolved in the Amœba by chemical processes and absorbed by it as nourishment.   The Amœba multiplies by division into two when it grows to a certain size, and it is often very abundant among dead leaves in a rain-pool.   There are many kinds or species of Amœba, of which that here figured is a sample.

Now we turn to the " phagocytes," the colourless corpuscles of the blood. They are parts or units of the actual substance of the multicellular animals in which they are abundant, and *not* parasites which have made their way in from the outside. Indeed, as we shall see, they are a sort of special guard or defence of the animal body against foreign intruders—such as Bacteria, Trypanosomes, and other " germs " which constantly make more or less effectual attempts to get into that little

Fig. 7.—Successive changes of form of a Colourless Corpuscle or " Phagocyte " from the Blood of Man—as seen through a high-power microscope on a glass plate kept at the temperature of the human body. The phases are about five seconds of time apart.

fortress, a living animal. In Fig. 7 we have represented a " phagocyte " from the blood of man. It is much smaller than the Amœba—twenty times smaller than the large one photographed—though Amœbæ as small are common. The same movements and change of shape are seen as in Fig. 5. The " phagocytes " are very abundant in human blood—there are 500 millions of them in a pint of it, but the " red corpuscles " are far more numerous—in the proportion of 5000 to 1. In Fig. 8 a " phagocyte " from the frog's blood is drawn from the life. It is larger and even more active than that of man.

Such " phagocytes " are abundant constituents of

3

the blood and lymph-like fluids of all animals. Sixty years ago it was shown that if some powdered vermilion is put into a drop of blood, the " phagocytes " (which were then called merely " white blood corpuscles ") will engulf the fine grains of vermilion—as an Amœba engulfs food-particles. But nothing came of this observation until three great discoveries were made—namely, (1) that infective diseases are caused by bacteria (Bacilli, Spirilla, and Cocci) which make their way from the exterior into the blood and tissues of healthy animals, and

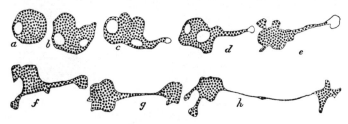

Fig. 8.—Successive changes of form of a Colourless Corpuscle or Phagocyte of the Frog's Blood, carefully drawn from life. The corpuscle is seen to be in process of fission or dividing into two (Fig. *h*). The phases of change drawn are separate from each other by about five seconds.

multiplying there produce the specific poisons of the diseases (fevers, etc.) of which they are the causes (Pasteur), and that the deadly suppuration of wounds is also due to intrusive Bacteria (Lister) ; (2) that the colourless corpuscles push their way through the wall of the finest blood-vessels when " inflammation " occurs at a wounded or injured part of the body (see Fig. 9, and its explanation), and accumulate by millions in the injured tissue (Cohnheim) ; (3) that in transparent water-fleas and marine animals infected by intrusive germs or foreign particles, one can actually *watch* the colourless blood corpuscles engorging and destroying the infective foreign particles in great numbers (Metchnikoff). It was Metchnikoff who brought these three facts together and connected them by his doctrine of " phagocytosis " —the special activity and significance of the hitherto un-explained colourless corpuscles of the blood to which he now gave the name " eater-cells " or " phagocytes." He showed by prolonged experiments and observations on all kinds of animals, healthy and diseased, that the business of the amœba-like phagocytes of the blood and lymph of animals is to swallow and destroy all intrusive germs and also to remove dead tissue and hurtful foreign bodies. In Fig. 6, B, we see a " phagocyte " engulfing and digesting a fever-causing " spirillum " in the blood of a guinea-pig —just as an Amœba engulfs its attractive food-particle (Fig. 6, A).

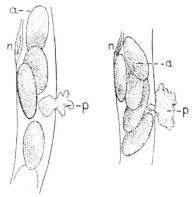

FIG. 9.—The out-wandering of a Phagocyte through the delicate wall of a blood-vessel (capillary) of the Frog. *a.*, the oval red blood corpuscles of the frog inside the blood-vessel. *p.*, the phagocyte. *n.*, nucleus of a cell of the wall of the capillary vessel.

In the left-hand figure the phagocyte has penetrated half-way to the exterior of the vessel. In the right hand figure it has very nearly got completely through. (From Metchnikoff.)

In Fig. 9 (*bis*) we see Metchnikoff's drawing of a large " phagocyte " which has engulfed a number of cholera-bacilli. Just in the same way (as hundreds of observers have now shown) all kinds of disease germs and the deadly " wound-infecting " germs are seized and destroyed by the ever-active

" phagocytes." They are indeed the " scavengers " of the animal body. It is on them that we have to rely in our battle against infective diseases. Consequently Metchnikoff and his followers have made careful experiments and found out what will help and what will retard the " phagocytes " in their life-saving work. They not only swallow and digest hostile germs, but are attracted or repelled by them, conquer them by chemical poisons which they exude, and produce other chemical bodies of great importance (antitoxins). They can be assisted and strengthened by various artifices now discovered by medical science.

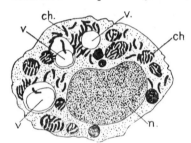

FIG. 9 (*bis*).—A large Phagocyte of the Guinea-Pig, which has engulfed many cholera microbes or " comma-bacilli," and is in course of digesting them. *ch.*, some of the cholera microbes. *n.*, the cell-nucleus of the phagocyte. *v.*, vacuity or liquid-holding cavities. (From Metchnikoff.)

The escape of the " phagocytes " (Fig. 9) from the blood-vessels in inflammation (" diapedesis," or " out-wandering," as it was called), and in fact inflammation itself, is explained by Metchnikoff. It only occurs in animals which have a highly developed system of blood-vessels *under the control of the nervous system.* The heat and redness of inflammation is due to a local arrest or congestion of the blood-stream, caused by a dilatation of the smaller veins under the control of special muscles and nerves. This local congestion of the blood-stream *allows the " phagocytes " to escape at an injured spot in vast numbers* (see Fig. 9), and so to eat up and destroy dead tissue, foreign substances, and, above all, the " wound - poisoning " bacteria, which would otherwise, having entered at the broken skin-surface, multiply with deadly effect. Thus we have briefly set forth the answer to the question "What are 'phagocytes'?" They are so important and are so dominant a feature in the new surgery and new medicine associated with the great germ-theory of disease, that every one should have a clear conception of their nature. Our knowledge of them has been greatly advanced by the study of wounds and their infection during the Great War, and is increasing every day.

CHAPTER IV

SOME POND-SNAILS

SNAILS are of many and various kinds. In drawing up the great pedigree of animals which is called " the classification of the animal kingdom," naturalists place them, with other creatures like them in structure, as a stem or great line of descent which is called the " Mollusca." It comprises the snails and whelks as well as the bivalve mussels, clams, and oysters. Examples of other great stems are the Vertebrates, the Appendiculates, the Starfishes.

The molluscs, as their name suggests, are remarkable for the softness of the body, which in most of them is protected by a hard shell or pair of shells. The body is not merely soft, but curiously elastic—so that it can change in shape, swelling out in one part and shrinking in another. The swelling is due to the driving of the blood from one region, of which the muscular wall contracts, into another which yields and becomes " taut," distended and expanded by the abundant blood. By this squeezing in one part and distension in another, the mollusc can force its head and body far beyond its shell, or again shrink rapidly out of view into the protecting shell.

This kind of expansion and contraction of the body is not seen in other animals except in the sea-anemones and the little polyps allied to them, where, however, the liquid which effects the expansion is not the animals' blood (they have no blood !), but sea-water taken in at the mouth. Lovers of the seashore and its curious inhabitants delight themselves by placing a sea-anemone —picked up on the rocks at low tide as a hard, fleshy lump as big as a large walnut—in a glass of sea-water. Slowly it takes water into itself through its mouth and expands as it relaxes its muscles, and after an hour or two is seen as a beautifully coloured little tower crowned with a circlet of delicate pointed tentacles of varied tint which surround the mouth. It has expanded to ten times its original bulk—and is, in fact, distended with the sea-water taken into it, and is " taut " and firm. Touch it now with your finger, and it shrinks ; it contracts as you watch it, driving out the sea-water from its mouth and the tips of its tentacles until it becomes the shapeless little fleshy lump with which you started.

This use of liquid to distend, and at the same time make firm and rigid, the soft, flaccid body is common to the polyps and to the molluscs ; and until a few years ago it was thought that the molluscs, like the polyps and sea-anemones, take in water into their blood-vessels so as to effect their expansion, and that they let it escape when they again shrink. But I was able to show at that time that molluscs do not take water into their blood when they expand themselves, nor throw out any liquid when they shrink. In a very few exceptional molluscs the blood is red, and one can see it driven into the expanding parts of the body, and also see that *none of the red blood escapes from the body as it contracts*. By careful measurement in a glass jar it has been shown that none of the water around it is taken into the blood-vessels when the mollusc expands, and that no liquid is thrown out by it

when it shrinks. The liquid in the body—the blood—
merely passes from one part of the animal which shrinks
to another part which expands. The shrinking part is
within the shell, and hidden by it, whilst the swelling

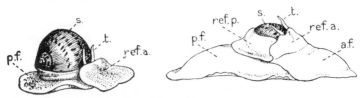

FIG. 10.—The Sea-Snail called Natica. In the left-hand figure it is
seen causing its foot and head gradually to swell out, by squeezing
the blood from the part of the body still concealed by the shell
into those regions (foot and head) which in consequence slowly
issue from the shell, although previously completely hidden
within it.

In the right-hand figure the process of swelling has been carried
further, so that the extruded regions are further distended
and almost completely spread over and conceal the shell. Yet
if the animal is now roughly touched or handled, the swollen
region quickly shrinks or " contracts " : the blood is driven from
them into that part of the body lying within the shell, and the
whole of the extruded part of the animal in half a minute
shrinks into the cavity of the shell and is completely hidden in and
protected by it. The reference letters have the following significance : *s.*, the shell ; *t.*, the pair of head-tentacles ; *p.f.*, the hinder
part of the expanding muscular " foot " by which the snail
crawls ; *a.f.*, the front part of the crawling foot ; *ref.a.*, the
reflected lobe of the front part of the foot ; *ref.p.*, the reflected
lobe of the hinder region of the foot which, together with the
reflected lobe of the front part, swells out over the shell so as
to envelope it almost completely, as shown in the right-hand
figure.

part emerges from the mouth of the shell. When that
extended part is withdrawn into the shell it drives the
blood which had distended it, back into the previously
shrunken part of the animal concealed in the shell, and
thus collapses and shrinks, far into the cavity of the
shell.

The common pond-snail, shown in Fig. 11, is readily found in any large pond of stagnant water crawling on the leaves of water-plants. It shrinks suddenly into its delicate spiral shell and is lost to view when caught; but, if kept in a jar of water, may be watched gradually swelling out from its shell, and crawling, as shown in the drawings here printed which I made a long time ago from some taken in the large ponds at Hampstead Heath. One sees that the expanded animal shows **a**

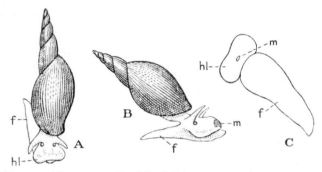

FIG. 11.—The common Pond-Snail, Limnæa stagnalis. Crawling.
f., foot ; *h.l.*, head lobes ; *m.*, mouth.
A, seen from above. B, side view. C, view of the crawling surface.
The eyes and head-tentacles are seen in A and B. Natural size.

large oblong pointed "*foot*," as it is called (*f.*), on the flat surface of which it crawls (Fig. 11, C), whilst raised on this cushion we see the " *head*," formed by two rounded lobes right and left (Fig. 11, A, *h.l.*), between which is the mouth (*m.*). The head carries a pair of pointed tentacles, and also, close by them, a pair of eyes. Behind the head, rising from the upper surface of the foot, is the " visceral hump." This remains always within and protected by the shell, which covers it and is firmly attached to it. The expanded animal is seen in B, hanging by a narrow stalk or connecting isthmus from the visceral mass con-

cealed in the shell. One cannot have a better example
of the soft mobile body of a mollusc than is given by
this beautiful semi-transparent pond-snail.

And now as to some other features of importance in
Mollusca. All of them except the bivalves (mussels,
oysters, cockles) have a very curious and elaborate rasp-
like plate within the mouth (Fig. 12). It grows from the
floor of the mouth, as a finger-nail grows at the end of
our fingers, and wears away as it is used. It is beset
with minute sharp teeth in rows of definite shape and

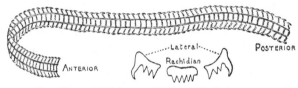

FIG. 12.—The Lingual Ribbon or " Tongue " of the common Whelk,
magnified about four diameters, showing its rasping teeth set
in rows of three. Below is drawn a single row of three teeth,
more highly magnified. The common pond-snail has a shorter
lingual ribbon, armed with smaller and more numerous teeth.

pattern (beautiful to look at with the microscope), comparable to the teeth on a rasp. It works up and down
across the opening of the mouth, being provided with
a ball-like mass of red-coloured muscles elaborately
disposed so as to give it vigorous and effective action.
It enables the molluscs provided with it to rasp down
vegetable and animal bodies which serve them as food ;
and in many cases even to bore holes through the shells
of other molluscs and so to feed on the soft animal within.
It is thus that the whelks attack and devour oysters.
You can see the pond-snail using his rasp, just visible
within his lips, as he crawls over the green growth on
the glass sides of an aquarium. The rasp-bearing

molluscs—the snails, slugs, whelks, periwinkles, limpets, and cuttle-fish—form a natural group of blood-relations, characterized by the possession (the common inheritance) of this remarkable organ, and separated from the bivalve molluscs—the two-shelled mussels, clams, oysters, and cockles—which are devoid of it. The bivalves swallow very minute microscopic floating plants (Diatoms and such-like) carried into their mouths by streams of water drawn there by the innumerable vibrating hairs or cilia with which their large gill-plates (the so-called " beard " of the oyster) are closely covered.

If we leave aside the very peculiar cuttle-fish, with their eight or ten arms beset with hooks and suckers, the rasp-bearing molluscs are all very much like our common pond-snail. They are all classed as " Gastropods," because their lower surface or belly is developed into a crawling foot, as we have seen in the pond-snail. The fresh-water and land-dwelling snails are derived from marine ancestors ; and some are specially adapted to breathe air. The marine kinds, such as whelks and periwinkles, have a pair of comb-like or feather-like *gills* protected by a hood or fold of the body. Usually this pair of gills is reduced to a single one. The gastropods have nearly all become lop-sided or one-sided. The origin of this lop-sidedness is connected with the *spiral* twist of the shell, as seen in our pond-snail (Fig. 11). It is a right or left " screw," as the case may be. Sometimes the spire is not drawn out, but is flat like a watch-spring, as in the flat-coiled pond-snail Planorbis (Fig. 13), which is common in ponds, living side by side with the other which is called Limnæa (Fig. 11). Both Planorbis and Limnæa are devoid of even one gill or gill-comb, and, like the land-snail (Helix) and land-slug (Limax), have the hood, which in other snails protects the gill-plume, converted into a chamber with small aperture capable of complete closure by muscles. You may easily see this aperture in the common garden snail and in the garden slug when it is crawling. This chamber contains air, and is a lung. Hence these snails are called the " Pulmonate Gastropods." There are fish which live in rivers liable to dry up, and, like the

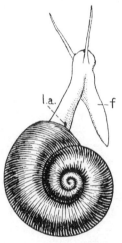 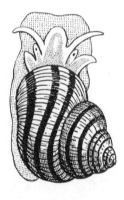

Fig. 13.—Flat-coiled Pond-Snail, Planorbis corneus. About twice the natural size.

Fig. 14.—Running water Pond-Snail, Paludina vivipara. About twice the natural size.

Pulmonate snails, have what is a gill-chamber in other fishes converted into a lung or air-breathing sac.

The shape of the shells of Pulmonate Gastropods differs in different kinds, as it does in the marine kinds. The whelks have long spiral shells like Limnæa, but heavier and stronger ; and some of the sea-snails have short spires like the garden snail, or they may have flat-coiled shells like Planorbis. The limpet is a marine snail with a simple cap-like or cup-like shell, without spire. In our mountain streams there lives a little Pulmonate snail similar in structure to Limnæa, but having a simple cap-like shell on its " visceral hump " like that of a limpet. It is called Ancylus, and is fairly common. There are also Pulmonate water-snails, which have a very minute spire to their shells, most of the shell consisting of a great open chamber out of proportion to the spire. These shells are intermediate in form between those of the common pond-snail and the cap-like one of Ancylus. They also live in running water, and constitute a genus called Physa. There are many species of Physa and many of Limnæa.

In Fig. 14 I have given a drawing of a very different kind of pond-snail, called Paludina. It is common enough, but will not live in stagnant water—a little streamlet must run through the pond in which it flourishes. I used to get it, with other stream-loving molluscs (e.g. the little bivalve " Cyclas "), in the " Leg of Mutton Pond " at Hampstead, which is the source of a small river, but it was not to be found in the great stagnant ponds of " the lower Heath." It has a fine striped snail-like shell, a big crawling foot, tentacles, and eyes raised on short stalks. It is not one of the Pulmonata, but has a gill plume, and by it breathes the oxygen—not of the air, but that dissolved in water. Its ancestors took to fresh water and left the sea at a later period than those of the Pulmonate pond-snails and allied land-snails. One great point of difference which separates it from the Pulmonates is that it possesses an *operculum*—a round horny shield growing on the hinder part of the foot, which fits tightly to the mouth of the shell when the animal withdraws into that chamber. Most of the sea-snails and whelks possess an *operculum*, but none of the

Pulmonates, with one doubtful exception, possesses it Some of the fresh-water operculate snails, allied to Paludina, have left the water altogether and taken to a life on land. They, like the Pulmonates, have lost the gill, and

Fig. 15.—Cyclostoma elegans, a land-living *operculate* Snail as seen when expanded from its shell and crawling. *op.*, the horny plate called the "operculum," which closes the mouth of the shell when the snail withdraws itself into that protective chamber. Natural size.

Fig. 16.—A Snail (closely allied to Cyclostoma) withdrawn into its shell, which is seen to be closed by the spirally-marked operculum, *op.*

breathe air through the wall of the gill-chamber, but they still keep the *operculum*. "Cyclostoma" is the name of one commonly to be found crawling on walls built of limestone rock in Gloucestershire (see Figs. 15 and 16).

CHAPTER V

POND-SNAILS AND BLOOD-RED

THE blood of man is red, owing to the fact that it consists of almost equal parts of a clear, nearly colourless liquid and of minute muffin-shaped corpuscles floating in the liquid. There are about 30,000 million of them in a spoonful of blood. These " corpuscles " are soft and semi-liquid. Each measures 1–3200th of an inch across, and consists of a red-coloured transparent substance called " blood-red," or " hæmoglobin," mixed with a nearly equal quantity of " slimy " white-of-egg-like material. The blood-red hæmoglobin can be dissolved by water, and will then separate from it as crystals of pure " hæmoglobin," which are called " blood-crystals." They differ a little in shape according to the species of animal from the blood of which they are obtained. Some are drawn here in Fig. 18. All mammals (warm-blooded quadrupeds), birds, reptiles, and fishes have red blood which owes its colour to the blood-crystals or hæmoglobin of " red-blood-corpuscles " which float in their blood.

Until fifty-five years ago we knew little more of this " hæmoglobin," and it seemed as though it existed only to give its noble colour to the blood, and to show through the skin in the healthy blush of the cheek, the coral-red of the human lips and of the cock's comb and of the turkey's wattles—also, perhaps, to betray by the redness of man's nose an unhealthy state of the circulation ! It is a very complex but definite chemical body—a chemical union of the elements carbon, nitrogen, oxygen, hydrogen, and sulphur with a small but definite quantity of iron.   Then it was studied by aid of the spectroscope, and its real significance revealed.

It is proverbial that one cannot trust to colour as a means of recognizing a given substance—*Ne crede colori*. You can make a solution in water of carmine and a little yellow pigment which to the unaided eye will pass for a solution of blood-crystals. Many other red solutions look like it ; and so with yellow, green, and blue substances—you cannot be sure what they are by their colour alone. If you allow white sunlight to pass through a prism you separate its " trains " and spread them out as the colours of the rainbow. You can so arrange that the white light coming through a narrow slit into a dark chamber shall be spread out as it passes through a prism of glass into an elongated band in which the red, yellow, green, blue, and purple " trains " of light which are mixed in white light are separated and follow one another in that order, one passing gradually into the next. This band of rainbow colours is called " the spectrum " (Fig. 17, top). Now, if you put a glass tube containing a coloured solution in front of the slit where the white sunlight enters the otherwise dark chamber, you find, as you would expect, that a red liquid lets the red pass, but stops—in fact, is " opaque " to—the other colours more or less ; a green liquid stops all or nearly all but the green ; a blue all but the blue. The " stopped " colours are simply *absorbed*, and where they were seen in the spectrum of white light it is now black and dark. Few, if any, red-coloured liquids absorb *exactly* the same extent or part of the spectrum ; nor are all yellow, or all green, or all blue liquids exactly alike in this matter. Their minor differences of " tint " are due to their absorbing or else letting pass more or less of the light of another colour. A very curious and important fact was discovered when various transparent coloured bodies (liquids and solids) were tested in this way. It was found that some (but by no means all) transparent coloured bodies cause *detached* black bands of absorption in the spectrum (see Fig. 17). They are called

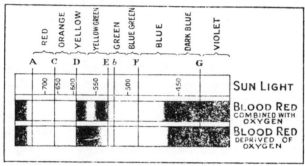

Fig. 17.—To show the " Absorption Bands " seen in the " Spectrum " of Sunlight which has passed through a weak solution in water of Blood-Red or Hæmoglobin.

" absorption *bands*," and can be accurately measured and their exact position in the spectrum fixed. Such coloured bodies as give detached absorption bands can be recognized and identified with absolute certainty by the position of those bands in the spectrum. As shown in Fig. 17, records of them are kept by which their position is shown as compared with that of certain fine dark lines always present in the spectrum of sunlight, called after their discoverer, " Fraunhofer's lines," and named by letters, as seen in Fig. 17. And even more exactly the wave-lengths of the trains of light

4

absorbed are ascertained. The figures 700 to 450 in the diagram of the spectrum of sunlight in Fig. 17 give the wave-lengths of the light-waves of each part of the spectrum in very minute units—namely, units of 1–10,000th of a millimetre—and thus we can fix and state once for all the position of any " absorption bands," so that the substance producing them can be unerringly recognized when its presence is suspected. The purple solution of a compound of the element manganese (known as Condy's fluid) gives six detached " absorption bands " in the green and blue part of the spectrum ; leaf-green, or chlorophyll, gives a remarkable series of separate absorption bands, and very many coloured bodies derived from plants and from animals give each their own special and readily recognized set of " absorption bands." Each can be recognized with certainty by these bands, and the position of the bands exactly measured, so that even a minute drop of a weak solution of such a colouring matter is sufficient for decisive examination, though chemical analysis would be hopeless as a means of recognition.

In 1864 Sir George Stokes, of Cambridge, found that a solution in water of blood-red or hæmoglobin gives two well-marked absorption bands in the yellow and green part of the spectrum (Fig. 17). When the blood of man or other animal has passed through the lungs it becomes bright red ; but, *before* being exposed in the lungs to the oxygen of the inspired air, it is dark and somewhat purple. It was found that a watery solution of hæmoglobin in a glass test-tube, if shaken up with air, becomes bright red, just as does the blood in the lungs, and that it loosely combines with or holds the oxygen gas of the air. It is then that it shows the two absorption bands (Fig. 17). But if the loosely combined

oxygen be taken away from the solution of hæmoglobin—a removal which can be easily brought about
by adding to the solution a few drops of a certain oxygen-
seizing chemical—then the hæmoglobin solution becomes
of a bluer purple hue, and, when examined with the
" spectroscope " (a convenient arrangement of slit and
prism to produce a spectrum), is found to give no longer
two absorption bands, *but only one*, not identical with
either of the two previously there (see Fig. 17). Now,
if we shake up the purple-looking deoxygenized solution
of hæmoglobin with a little air, it at once takes up some
oxygen and becomes bright red again, and again shows
two absorption bands in the spectrum. And we can
again take away the oxygen with the deoxidizing chemical
and make it purple and one-banded, and again brighten
it with oxygen, and so keep on ringing the changes.
In fact, the hæmoglobin becomes bright-red two-banded
oxy-hæmoglobin by taking up oxygen, and " reduced "
or simple one-banded claret-coloured hæmoglobin when
deprived of that oxygen. And so we have the explanation
of its presence in the blood. The hæmoglobin or blood-
red is there as a *condenser* and *carrier of oxygen*, taking up
that gas as it passes through the lungs and conveying it
to the most distant parts of the body, where it is largely
given up to the living tissues more greedy of it than the
blood-red itself, which returns, darkened in tint, in the
veins to the heart, and so once more to the lungs for a
fresh supply of oxygen and a renewal of its bright colour.

The discovery of the absorption bands of hæmoglobin
has enabled us to recognize its presence in various small
animals and in unexpected parts of the body. It has thus
been shown that the red colour of meat—that is, of
animals' muscle—is due to the presence of hæmoglobin
in the muscular fibre, not to blood in their blood-vessels.

The muscles require much oxygen, and the hæmoglobin of the muscular fibre holds it and stores it. Many marine worms and the earth-worms and river-worms have beautiful networks of blood-vessels, the blood in which is red. It is proved that this is due to hæmoglobin in solution, by the absorption bands produced by it in the spectroscope and by the crystals which it forms. Insects and spiders and such creatures as crabs, lobsters, and shrimps, with rare exceptions, have no hæmoglobin ; neither their blood nor their muscles are red. Nor have the molluscs red blood or red muscles, with rare and curious exceptions. And so we are brought back to the flat-coiled pond-snail (Planorbis corneus) of which I wrote in the last chapter (Fig. 13). It is one of these exceptions. It was long known to eject a dark red fluid from its body when cut or pricked. I examined this red fluid with the spectroscope, and proved conclusively that the colour was due to hæmoglobin and that the fluid was the snail's blood. The common long-shelled pond-snail (Limnæa) (Fig. 11) has colourless or pale-bluish blood, and so have all other molluscs, except two or three of the bivalves. Here, then, we are brought by the pond-snails to this puzzling and interesting question— Why should the flat-coiled pond-snail have a rich stock of the oxygen-carrier hæmoglobin in its blood, and the other snails have none ? And yet another startling fact is revealed by the spectroscope when used to explore the colours of snails. The little globular mass of muscles which moves the pond-snail's rasp-like tongue is [of a pale red colour : in marine snails it is actually of a rich *ruby*-red. All the other muscles of these snails are colourless and the blood in all, except Planorbis, is colourless or very pale blue. Yet this pink or ruby-red ball of rasp-muscles was shown when I examined it with the spectroscope to owe its colour to hæmoglobin—the very same red oxygen-carrying blood-crystals which we find in the red corpuscles and the muscular fibre of man and the great animals allied to him ! It seems that hæmoglobin can quite exceptionally be present in some animals and in some parts of animals, and not in others ; but it is difficult to connect its presence in all cases with any obvious and special need for it. I found it in the nerve cord of a marine worm, the " sea-mouse," which it stains bright crimson, although there is none in that worm's blood. Some water-fleas (Crustacea) living in stagnant ponds have it dissolved in their blood ; and so—absolutely alone among insects—has the ruby-red larva of the harlequin-fly (Chironomus), which lives in the black foul mud of ponds, where oxygen must be a rare and precious commodity. Boys used to call it a " blood-worm," and use it as a bait to catch sticklebacks.

The blood of lower animals, which does not possess the red oxygen-carrying hæmoglobin—including that of most of the mollusca and the insects, spiders, scorpions, and crustacea (crabs and lobsters and shrimps) —has often a pale-blue oxygen-carrying substance in it instead. It is called Hæmocyanin, and is indigo-blue when carrying oxygen, and nearly colourless when deoxidized. It gives no detached absorption bands in the spectrum of light passed through it. Further, in some marine worms (the Chlorhæmians) the blood is *green* instead of red. This is due to a substance which I discovered in 1868 and called " chlorocruorin." It carries oxygen, and gives two peculiar absorption bands. Since red, blue, and green substances exist in the blood of different animals and act as oxygen-carriers, it is not improbable that special *colourless* oxygen-carrying substances also exist in the blood and tissues of animals which are colour less. A means of detecting and isolating such substances has yet to be discovered.

The fact that the hæmoglobin of different animals forms crystals of different shape in many instances (see

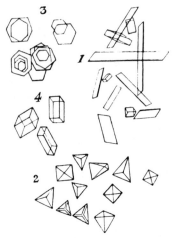

Fig. 18.—Crystals of the Red Colouring Matter of the Blood Corpuscles, known as " Blood-Red " or Hæmoglobin.
1, from the human blood.
2, from the rat's blood.
3, from the squirrel's blood.
4, from the blood of the hamster (a kind of rat).
The crystals are magnified a thousand times linear.

Fig. 18) shows that the hæmoglobin is not precisely identical in all cases. This fact has been carefully established, but whether other peculiarities accompany this difference in crystalline form, has not yet been ascertained,

CHAPTER VI

THE POND-SNAIL'S FLEA

A TINY, colourless, worm-like little creature lives on the surface of the bodies of both the elongate and the flat-coiled pond-snails (Limnæa and Planorbis). When you watch a pond-snail crawling or floating in a small dish of water over which you bend closely (with, if you like, a watchmaker's magnifying glass in your eye), you will see these minute worms, not more than one-sixth of an inch long, moving about on the snail's body, clinging to it by their hook-like bristles (Fig. 19, B) massed in paired bundles (Fig. 19, A, and Fig. 20, B). You can see them letting go their front hold so as to stretch the head and neck and take a more advanced grip, and draw the rest of the body forwards—somewhat in the same way as a looping caterpillar walks (Fig. 19, B). This little creature may well be called the pond-snail's " flea," as it infests the surface of the pond-snail's body much as fleas infest the higher animals—though it is not one of the six-legged " insects," as the flea is, but is one of the " bristle-footed " annulate worms, or Chætopoda, similar in structure to the earth-worm and many kinds of freshwater and marine worms.

I have found from four or five to as many as twenty of these little parasites on a single snail, and when I first made their acquaintance, many years ago while

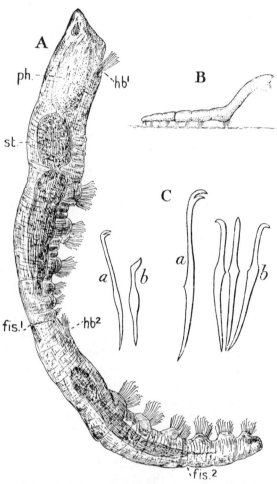

FIG. 19.—The little Worm, Chætogaster Limnææ, which lives like a flea on the body of the Pond-Snails, Limnæa and Planorbis.

A, a highly magnified view of the worm lying on its side. *ph.*, pharynx; *st.*, stomach; *h.b.*[1], head-bristle bundle of parent worm; *h.b.*[2], head-bristle bundle of second or budded worm; *fis.*[1], line of fission by which the second worm will separate from the first; *fis.*[2], second line of fission by which a third worm will separate from the second. *a*, ordinary hooked bristle; *b*, genital bristle or seta (club-shaped).

B, the worm crawling with upraised head.

C, *a*, ordinary hooked bristle, and *b*, genital bristles of the worm, Nais serpentina.

dissecting pond-snails, I determined to find out all I could about their life-history and structure, and year after year I kept an eye on them. They were called Chætogaster (signifying " bristled belly ") by their first discoverer. Two or three species (one nearly half an inch long) are known which live freely among the floating duck-weed of ponds, and are, as is also that frequenting the pond-snail, glass-like in their transparency, so that their digestive tract, brain, and nerves, blood-vessels and kidneys, muscles, etc., can be readily studied in living specimens with high powers of the microscope. The kind infesting the pond-snail was called Chætogaster Limnææ by the great naturalist Von Baer.

Our Fig. 19, A, shows the little worm picked up from the snail's body with the aid of a fine glass tube and placed on a slip of glass beneath the microscope. It is shown as it appears when lying on its side, and is magnified about forty times (linear). The specimens drawn in Fig. 20, A and B, are somewhat flattened by the pressure of a thin cover-glass ; they are lying on the back, and are magnified only twenty times (linear). In all three specimens the bundles of bristles (projecting in Fig. 19, A, from the belly) are the most arresting feature. The mouth is at the front end of the worm (*m.* in Fig. 20), and one sees the large pharynx and crop and gut of the digestive tract showing through the transparent body wall. The pair of bristle-bundles nearest to the mouth are called the " head-bristles " (*h.b.*) ; they are longer than those of the other " bundles " ; are more numerous, being twelve in each bundle instead of eight ; and are directed forward. The shape of a bristle with its double hook is shown in Fig. 19, A, *a*. The bristles are moved by muscles, and spread out like the spokes of a fan, clinging to or letting go of the snail's skin as required. The bristle-bundles of the head are separated by a considerable gap from the first pair of bristle-bundles of the " body," and these succeed one another at short intervals (see Figs. 19 and 20). Each pair of bristle-bundles indicates a " ring " or " segment " of the worm's body ; and the long gap between the head-bristle-bundles and the first of the body-bundles is due to the suppression of one or more pairs corresponding to intermediate " rings " or " segments." It will be seen in Fig. 19, A, that three pairs of well-grown bristle-bundles of the " body " region are succeeded by three or more pairs of quite small bristle-bundles, which are actually young and " sprouting." There is, in fact, a region of *new growth* following on the three well-grown bristle-bundles of the body region. We must remember that the little worm's body is like that of the earth-worm and other ringed or annulate worms—made up of a series of successive " rings " or " segments " not clearly marked off from one another in Chætogaster, but indicated by the pairs of bristle-bundles which succeed one another at intervals. Each pair, as in the earth-worm and the sea-worms, belongs to a distinct ring. Just as the pairs of bristle-bundles are repeated externally in successive rings, so are internal organs, such as the little kidneys (*nephridia*) and the blood-vessels and nerve-ganglia, repeated, each ring being thus a more or less exact repetition of those in front of and behind it.

That repetition of segments as " units of structure " is the characteristic of the annulated animals. Often in the Chætopoda, also called Annelids or annulated worms, the successive constituent rings or segments are over a hundred in number (150 in a big earth-worm), sometimes as few as twenty. Here in the little Chætogaster very few segments are held together to make up an individual.

It is obvious in both Fig. 19, A, and Fig. 20, B, that the chain of segments is *about to break into two*. A new head with head‑bristles has formed at the point marked *h.b.* between 3 and 2 in Fig. 20, B. You can see the new head also in Fig. 19, A, following the dark constriction near the middle of the chain. The rule appears to be that, following after every three pairs of body‑bristle‑bundles indicating three segments of the body, a region of "new growth" is formed in which not only a new head with its head‑bristles proceeds to take shape, but also new young bundles of bristles belonging to new rings which form

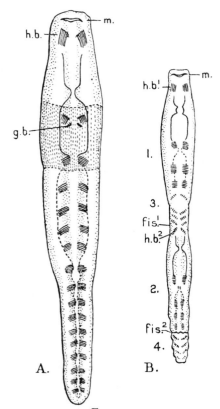

FIG. 20.

A, adult completed form of Chætogaster Limnææ, showing *h.b.*, head-bristles; *g.b.*, genital bristles; *m.*, mouth, and sixteen pairs of ordinary bristles. No regions of new growth or fission are present.

B, fissiparous larval or young stage of the same, showing two sets of head-bristles *h.b.*[1] and *h.b.*[2], and two lines of fission *fis.*[1] and *fis.*[2]. Two more advanced individuals, 1 and 2, and two less advanced, 3 and 4, budded respectively from them, are seen, constituting a rapidly growing chain, which will continue to grow in the same manner and break into separate individuals.

between the new head and the third ring or body-bristle-bundle of the front or leading worm. You thus get continually going on an " intercalation " of new growth at definite points in the chain, and a breaking of the chain into two when a new " head " is sufficiently grown to act as such for the rings behind it. In Fig. 20, B, this history is marked out by the successive numbers 1, 3, 2, 4. Between 1 and 2, which *were originally continuous*, a new growth of rings or segments (labelled 3) has taken place. Also behind 2 a new growth (labelled 4) is proceeding. The head of 2 (indicated by the head-bristles *h.b.* and the long gap following them) is nearly complete, and then " fission " or division will occur just in front of $h.b.^2$. The front individual consisting of 1 and 3 is already far advanced in the growth of new rings between it and the head of the separating individual marked by the letters $h.b.^2$ In its own hinder region (labelled 4) this new individual is far advanced in the production of new rings and bristle-bundles for further separation as distinct individuals. This process of intercalation of new segments and subsequent fission is seen, with special variations and laws as to the number of segments involved, in other annulate worms—for instance, in the freshwater Nais and the marine Syllis. The reader should now turn to Fig. 22 (*bis*) and its explanation.

The chains of Chætogaster Lymnææ grow and multiply by fission in this way during all the spring and summer. In early spring they are found even *inside* the pond-snail in its kidney as well as on its surface. But, like all other animals, Chætogaster has, we may be sure, another mode of multiplication—namely, by detaching from its body microscopic egg-cells which are fertilized by microscopic sperms. Such " eggs," in the case of other worms, are often laid in egg-capsules, from which they hatch as very minute microscopic young. For three years I searched for this phase of the life-history of Chætogaster at all seasons, and at last I found, in the first week of one October, my elusive little acquaintance in his adult full-blown condition.   At that date one or two of the " wormlets " (so we may designate Chæto-gaster), crawling on a freshly caught pond-snail, were seen by me to be larger by one-third or more than their companions.   In ever-renewed hope of finding the pond-snail's wormlet in its adult condition, I examined one of these larger specimens under the microscope, and what I saw is sketched in Fig. 20, A.   I had at last run down the full-grown adult stage of the Chætogaster Limnææ.   Natur-ally enough, in accordance with its increase in size, the little worm had abandoned its prolific habit of inter-calating new heads in its chain of segments and of breaking into two whenever a new head was complete. Now the worm consisted of a head

Fig.   21. — Fan-like Bundle of Bristles, twenty-two in num-ber, from the head-region of the adult or sexually mature Chætogaster Lim-nææ.

region with a pair of large head-bristle-bundles, followed by sixteen pairs of body-bristle-bundles, set at regular intervals and indicating sixteen constituent rings or segments of the body.   I soon discovered other speci-mens of this construction.   The bristles in all the bundles were *larger* and *twice as numerous* as those in the " fissiparous " or immature form (Fig. 21).   More-over, as shown in Fig. 20, A, a thickening of the skin formed a girdle just over that part *g.b.* where the crop or stomach shows through it.   This thickened girdle occurs in the earth-worm and many fresh-water worms

where it is known as the *clitellum*, and secretes a ring-
like case in which the eggs are enclosed when laid.

The most important fact which I found was that in
this, the adult or sexually ripe form, a new pair of bristle-
bundles (*g.b.*) has made its appearance in the neck-like
" gap " between the head-bristles and the earlier first
pair of body-bristle-bundles. This indicates the development of a previously dormant
region or segment in which
the essential generative products — the egg - cells or
" ova," and the sperms and
the sacs connected with
fertilization, known in other
worms as " spermathecæ,"
or sperm-receptacles—were, I
found, now present. On the
surface four of the bristles
on each side (*g.b.*) had grown
of a new shape—they were
short, blunt " clubs," instead
of being double-hooks as that
in Fig. 19. I subsequently
found other specimens of the

FIG. 22.—The uncleft " Genital "
Bristles of an adult Chætogaster
Limnææ, growing close to the
first pair of abdominal bristle-
bundles, and indicating the
formation here of a new segment, the genital segment
shown in Fig. 20, A, and not
present in the fissiparous immature worms drawn in Fig. 20, B.

adult wormlet on my pond-snails ; and also found in a
beautiful snake-like worm (Nais serpentina) an inch long,
coiling round dead twigs in a neighbouring pond, that
the same change from a fissiparous or dividing *young*
or *larval* form to a non-dividing *adult sexual* form
occurs, and that as in Chætogaster, so in Nais, a new
segment grows into place in the neck region when the
adult stage is attained, that in it the ova and sperms,
etc., develop, and that this segment has peculiar short
club-shaped bristles not present in the immature fissi-

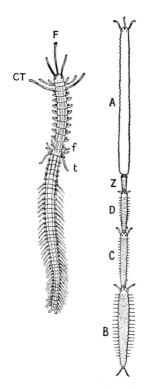

Fig. 22 (*bis*).—Fission of Marine Annelids. The left-hand figure shows
the worm known as Autolytus cornutus—one of the "Syllids"—
dividing into two individuals of differing character; the anterior
is sexless, but the hinder is a ripe male, distinguished by the
name "Polybostrichus."   The legs and bristle-bundles of the
parent worm are totally unlike those of the hinder worm now
about to separate as an independent individual.   F and CT,
tentacles and tentacular cirri of the a-sexual parent worm; *f* and
t, those of the male about to break away.
The right-hand figure is a diagram showing the plan of bud-production
and fission in many marine-worms called Syllids.   A is the parent
a-sexual worm; Z is the zone of growth of new segments which
does not give rise to merely *one* sexual individual, but is continuously producing new individuals, B, C, D—the oldest, B, is the
farthest from the zone of new growth.   The new individuals are
unlike the parent worm A, and are sexual.   Compare this
arrangement with that shown by Chætogaster, Fig. 20, A and B.

parous worm. These bristles I called the "genital setæ." So it was established (for the first time), and has since been confirmed by other naturalists, that in these little freshwater annelids or annulose worms there is a *larval* fissiparous form which gives rise, after multiplying for a season by fission, to an adult sexual form differing considerably from the larva especially in size, the absence of fission, and the presence of a hitherto suppressed genital segment carrying the reproductive organs and peculiar club-shaped genital setæ. Up to the present date (1922) no one has seen the eggs of the Chætogaster when fertilized and laid, nor has the development of the young worm from the egg been described.

Now that I have said as much as I think the reader will, for the moment, care to read about the pond-snail's flea or wormlet, I wish to emphasize the fact that one can readily observe so much that is remarkable and of wide significance in a common pond-snail. In the three articles which I have devoted to it I have merely sketched some of the more obvious of these things which any one can readily verify, if he will venture so far as to keep three or four pond-snails in a basin of water. In the next chapter I shall tell of a very curious and important matter concerning pond-snails—namely, their relation to that terrible pest of the farmer, " sheep-rot."

CHAPTER VII

THE LIVER-FLUKE

T HE liver-fluke [1] is shown of its natural size in our drawing, Fig. 23, A. Its occurrence in sheep was first described in 1547 : it causes a diseased condition in them which is called " sheep-rot." It has rarely been found in man : only twenty-eight cases are recorded. But all over the world it is a serious pest in sheep and oxen. In 1879, 300,000 sheep were killed by it in England alone, and in 1891 one owner lost 10,000 in this way. It inhabits the bile-ducts and, when numerous, causes atrophy of the liver by blocking its passages, and death results. It does not feed on the bile, but on the blood of its victim. Necessarily it became a matter of great importance to find out how the sheep become infected by this parasite, and, owing to the vast increase of our knowledge of parasites generally during the last century, many attempts were made to discover the life-history of the liver-fluke, but it was not until 1883 that this was accomplished by Mr. A. P. Thomas, a young student at Oxford, who anticipated the final work of the great parasitologist, Professor Leuckart, of Leipzig, who had long been busy in the quest. Mr. Thomas, as will be seen, rendered it possible by his discovery to protect sheep from this destructive disease.

[1] The name "Distomum" was given to it 150 years ago, because it seemed to have two mouths : the true mouth m in our figure A, and the ventral sucker s.

5

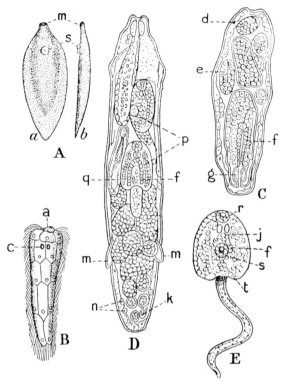

FIG. 23.—The life-history of the Liver-Fluke, Distomum hepaticum.

A, *a*, ventral, and *b*, lateral aspect of the adult worm from the sheep's liver. A little larger than life. *m*, mouth; *s*, ventral sucker.

B, the " miracidium," which hatches from the eggs of the liver-fluke, and swims freely in pond-water. *a*, mouth; *c*, eyes.

C, sporocyst, into which the miracidium is converted when it makes its way into the body of the little snail, Limnæa truncatula. *d*, the eyes degenerating; *e*, an internal bud or embryo; *f*, gut; and *g*, collar of young Redia, to which a bud has given origin.

D, fully formed Redia, one of several extruded from the sporocyst. *k*, germs growing into young Cercariæ; *m*, external lappets characteristic of Rediæ; *n*, germ-cells; *p*, young Cercariæ; *q*, young Redia.

E, freely swimming Cercaria, the tail-bearing young form of the liver-fluke. *r*, oral sucker; *s*, posterior sucker; *t*, granules; *j*, pharynx; *f*, gut.

The liver-fluke is one of a numerous group of parasites—but little known a hundred years ago—which
have a smooth, flat, oval body—varying in size from a
sixth of an inch to more than an inch in length—at one
end of which is a sucker-like mouth (Fig. 23, A, *m.*),
whilst one or more merely adhesive suckers (*s.*) are present
on other parts of the body—varying in number and
position in the different kinds. Other minute openings for
the renal organs and for the egg-ducts and sperm-ducts
are also present, but the large bifid gut, sometimes tree-
like and branched, has no posterior opening. Rudolphi,
in 1808, gave the name Trematoda—meaning " pierced
with holes " (Greek : τρηματώδης)—to the whole class
comprising these worms, distinguishing them from
other parasites known as " Tape-worms " and
" Thread-worms."

It became known in the middle of last century that
many parasitic worms have two " hosts " or animals
which they infest in turn—one during their young
condition, which is called the " primary host," and the
other the " final host," into which they pass in order to
finish their growth, become mature and lay their eggs.
The parasites usually pass from the first to the second
host readily enough owing to the fact that the final host
habitually preys upon the primary one—and so swallows
the young parasite with its hospitable entertainer. But
sometimes the parasite transfers itself by its own activity
and locomotion from the earlier host to the later. Also
very noteworthy facts are that only some *one* species of
animal, or its close allies, is possible as intermediate host,
and that there is usually also but a limited choice as to
the second or final host—it must be one of some two or
three particular species of animals which are in close
relation to the earlier host.

In many cases the young stage of the parasite which hatches from the egg of the adult can swim or crawl, and so get into the primary or intermediate host. But in the common tape-worm of man, called Tænia solium, it does not leave the egg-shell until it, and usually a whole lot of the eggs, contained in a joint or segment of a tape-worm, are swallowed by a pig—its usual primary host. The minute creature which issues from each egg is a little globe (1–200th of an inch across) armed with six hooks. By aid of these it bores into the blood-vessels of the pig's intestine and so is carried by the blood-stream into the muscles (flesh), where it is stopped by the narrowness of the fine blood-vessels. Here it (or rather " they," for usually there are some hundreds together) grows and becomes a little bladder as large as a big pea, and a curious little head consisting of a circular crown of many hooks and four suckers makes its appearance as an inward growth of each bladder. Pork infected with these little bladders is called " measled," and the bladders are called the " cysticercus " or " hydatid phase " of the tape-worm If eaten uncooked by a man (as happens where " raw meat " is a popular dish), the bladders are destroyed by mastication, but one or more of the little heads survive and adhere to the wall of the man's intestine by means of their suckers and crown of hooks. The adventurous young tape-worm has now fixed itself in its final host. It grows rapidly—absorbing the nutritive juices around it without the use of any mouth or digestive canal. It gives rise to a long, tape-like growth which consists of segments or joints continuously produced by the fixed " head." Those nearest the head are narrow and minute, but increase in size as they are pushed forward by the growth of new ones behind them. The string or " tape " becomes as much as 10 feet long, and consists of 850 joints or segments of which

the older—those farthest from the so-called " head "—
are three-quarters of an inch long and a third of an inch
broad. The oldest 400 joints are full of eggs, and those
at the free end continually break off and pass out of the
ntestine, each filled with many hundreds of eggs already
so far advanced in development as to contain six-hooked
embryos ready to be swallowed by a pig, and to recom-
mence the story with which we started above.

There are many variations of this story in different
kinds of tape-worms. There is a minute tape-worm
only a quarter of an inch long, which lives in a dog or
a wolf as its final host. The bladder stage (hydatid
or cysticercus phase), which develops from this tape-
worm's eggs, occurs in man and herbivorous animals.
A single cyst, or bladder, thus developed grows to an
enormous size—as big as a cocoa-nut—fixing itself,
when quite minute, in the liver or lung of its primary
host. Not one (as in cysts of measled pork) but many
hundred minute " heads " consisting of a crown of hooks
and four suckers are budded off within the cyst and float
there until it bursts and the victim usually dies. Then
there is a chance that a dog or a wolf will lick up some of
the liquid containing the floating heads, each capable of
growing in the dog's or wolf's intestine into a ripe, egg-
bearing little tape-worm. The " staggers " in sheep is
produced by the cystic or hydatid phase of another tape-
worm, which develops in the sheep's brain, whilst the
tape-worm matures in the sheep-dog—its final host. The
list of tape-worms and their hosts could be greatly extended and would include a variety of birds, reptiles,
and fishes as well as simpler invertebrate creatures. A
very striking feature is the enormous abundance either
of the eggs produced in the final stage, or if not of them,
then of the individual heads budded from a cyst in the

primary host. It is clear that the chances of any individual tape-worm born of an egg getting through his allotted course of life—reaching in due order, first the correct primary host and then, by the misfortune of that primary host in being eaten, the correct final host—are very small. And so the number of individuals produced and entering on the venture has to be enormous. Thousands, even hundreds of thousands, must start, in order that one or two may come triumphantly through to the final adult stage and reproduce themselves by eggs and sperm.

And now we return to the liver-fluke. Some of the Trematoda, to which group the flukes belong, are external parasites and cling with their suckers on to the gills of fishes. Others have only one host and venture as parasites only into the cavities of some aquatic animals, without presenting any striking peculiarities except in their elaborate suckers. The flukes, on the other hand—properly so called—have the mouth sucker and usually a second as in the liver-fluke (Fig. 23, A). The young hatched from the eggs of the adult, very unlike their parent, pass into a primary host—usually a mollusc—in which they multiply abundantly, producing strange forms, some of the offspring of which eventually get to the final host, usually a vertebrate, and, becoming adult, lay eggs.

In the case of the liver-fluke—Distomum hepaticum —the final host is the sheep—sometimes oxen and rarely man. The question has been (but now is solved), "What is the intermediate host and what is the history of the young fluke in connection with it ?" It has been long known that sheep in marshy pasture-land liable to be flooded, often become infected, and when, some fifty years ago, the history of some species of flukes which infest birds as their final host was traced to snails as primary hosts, it seemed likely that some kind of water-snail would prove to be the primary host of the liver-fluke of the sheep. The common pond-snails—Limnæa and Planorbis, of which I wrote in Chapter IV— were known to be attacked by the young hatched from the eggs of certain flukes (as many as eight kinds) which attain their adult condition in birds and other verte-brates. They hatch in fresh water when the fluke's eggs are passed from the birds, as minute, very active swimming creatures about the fiftieth of an inch long. These young swim about by means of a clothing of vibratile hairs and have a pair of eye-spots (Fig. 23, B). This young stage is called a " miracidium." The ciliated miracidia of some kinds of flukes when they happen to swim into the neighbourhood of an ordinary pond-snail (Limnæa stagnalis) seem to be drawn to it by a chemical attraction (smell or taste) and make their way into its soft body. Here they undergo a change of shape and increase in size, losing their coat of motile hairs. They produce young by internal budding (Fig. 23, C), which may in their turn multiply by internal budding and sooner or later produce a great number of curiously shaped worms, which are called " King's yellow worms " on account of their colour, or " Redia "—after the old Italian naturalist Redi, who described them but did not know their history. The Redia with its curious pair of lappets marked *m. m.* is shown in Fig. 23, D. The earlier forms are called " sporocysts." The Redia produces other Rediæ by internal budding, but also very soon, and as a final step before breaking up, the Redia produces *within* itself a number of minute tadpole-like creatures which are called Cercariæ. These escape from the snail and swim about in the water, lashing their tails (Fig. 23, E). The Cercaria is seen on examination to be nothing more than a minute fluke with circum-oral sucker (Fig. 23, E, *r*.), and a large hinder sucker (*s*.), though it is peculiar in possessing a lashing, active tail like that of a tadpole. The Cercaria, in one way or another (not fully made out in every case), manages to get swallowed by the bird which is its final host. Often the whole snail, with its stock of completed Cercariæ within it, is swallowed by the bird. Once inside the bird's stomach the Cercaria loses its tail and slowly grows to be an adult fluke. It was not until the particular kind of pond-snail requisite for these stages of development in the case of the liver-fluke was discovered that the whole history of that parasite could be traced. The ciliated young, or miracidia, of the liver-fluke are easily hatched from the eggs of that worm when it is ripe and removed from the liver of a dead sheep, but they were not attracted by the common pond-snail, Limnæa stagnalis, nor by the flat-coiled snail Planorbis, nor by other species such as Limnæa perigra and other kinds of snails. Under these circumstances Mr. Thomas examined the water-meadows near Oxford, where "sheep-rot" was frequent, and he found that after the floods had receded there were large numbers of a very small kind of pond-snail, about one-fifth of an inch long, known as Limnæa truncatula, adhering to the grass from which the water had disappeared. He collected a quantity of this small water-snail and brought them to the laboratory, where he had a glass basin in which hundreds of the ciliated miracidia hatched from the eggs of the sheep's fluke were swimming. I myself saw the experiment. He placed two or three of the little snails in the water. They expanded and began to crawl, but immediately, as though drawn by a magnet, the ciliated young or miracidia swam at them and violently pressed on to and into their bodies. The right snail was found at last! Mr. Thomas had then no difficulty in infecting a large number and following day by day the growth and changes which the little parasites undergo in the Limnæa truncatula. The chief of these are exhibited in Fig. 23, copied from the memoir published by Mr. Thomas in the " Quarterly Journal of Microscopical Science," 1883. I have already explained these figures, taking them to exhibit several features which are present in the whole group of " flukes." An important fact, observed long ago, but re-established by Mr. Thomas, is that the Cercariæ swimming in the flood waters as they recede, attach themselves, each in a sort of slimy case, to the blades of grass and so are eaten by the sheep when they return to the pasture. Numbers of the little pond-snails infested with the liver-fluke's Cercariæ, or tadpoles, are left high and dry on the grass, and may be eaten with the grass by the sheep unless removed or destroyed.

A very serious disease is caused in Africa by an elongated species of fluke which lives in the blood of man and is called Bilharzia. It has been shown that in this parasite also a water-snail serves as the intermediate host. I may, perhaps, point out that to prevent his sheep from being attacked by liver-fluke, the farmer (in Europe and Asia) must keep them away from meadows which have been recently flooded, and must also take steps to prevent the survival of the Limnæa truncatula up to the time when the flooded land is re-entered. In North and South America and the Sandwich Islands, other allied species of Limnæa are reported as acting the part of primary host to the liver-fluke, and in Australia a snail of the genus Bulimus is said to take it over. But detailed information is wanting.

CHAPTER VIII

PROGRESS!

THE word "progress" primarily signifies "a stepping forwards"—forwards not in relation to some real or imaginary goal the arrival at which we assume to be desirable, but merely in regard to the individual moving—in fact, a stepping "frontwards" as opposed to standing still or to stepping "backwards." In the course of the past few centuries it has, however, acquired a definite secondary limitation—that of the movement or development of human society towards a desirable goal—namely, earthly felicity, happiness, even perfection—or towards the attainment of perfect happiness in a future state of existence. The measure of "progress" thus necessarily has varied according to the conception of "happiness"—about which there have always been divergent opinions, and never an accepted definition. The philosophers of antiquity were pessimists : they did not entertain a belief in progress, but, on the contrary, held (with the notable exception of the Epicureans) that we are receding from a long-past golden age of happiness.

The notion of earthly progress was opposed by the Christian Church, which endeavoured to fix men's minds on a future state of rewards and punishments. A belief in the distribution of these by its intervention was the chief basis of the authority and power of the Church. The spirit of the Renaissance—the challenge to the authority of the ancients and of the Church, the emancipation of the natural man in the fields of art and of literature, and, later, in the sphere of philosophical thought—was accompanied by the development of the idea of progress. Ramus, a mathematician, writes in the year 1569 : " In one century we have seen a greater progress in men and works of learning than our ancestors had seen in the whole course of the previous fourteen centuries." The French historian, Jean Bodin, about the same time, reviewing the history of the world, was the first definitely to deny the degeneration of man, and comes (as Prof. Bury tells us in his fascinating book " The Idea of Progress ") nearer to the idea of progress than anyone before him. " He is," says Prof. Bury, " on the threshold." And then the Professor proceeds to trace through the writings of successive generations of later philosophers and historians—such as Le Roy, Francis Bacon, Descartes, the founders of the Royal Society, and others, such as Leibniz, Fontenelle, de Saint-Pierre, Montesquieu, Voltaire, Turgot, Rousseau, Condorcet, Saint-Simon, and Comte—the various forms which this idea of " progress " assumed, its expansions and restrictions, its rejection and its defence, until we come to the Great Exhibition of 1851—a demonstration and forecast (from a certain point of view) of progress— and, later still, to the new aspect given to the idea of progress by the doctrine of evolution and the theories of Darwin and of Spencer.

We are thus provided with a valuable history of an important line of human thought. But the most interesting part to many of us must be the closing pages in

which the actual state of the idea of progress as it appears
in the light of evolution is sketched, and the questions are
raised, which it has not been Prof. Bury's purpose to
discuss, namely, Granted that there has been progress,
in what does it consist ?   Is it likely to continue ?   Does
the doctrine of evolution, now so firmly established, lead
us to suppose that " progress " will continue, and, if so,
what will be its character ?   Or is it (however we define
it) coming to an end ?   Will stagnation, or will decay
and degeneration, as some suppose, necessarily follow ?
Or is " progress " (whatever one may mean by that
word) a law of human nature ?

The doctrine of the gradual evolution of the inorganic
universe had already gained wide acceptance before the
epoch when Darwin's " Origin of Species " brought man
into the area of evolution, and established the accepted
belief in the " progress " of man from an animal ancestry
to the present phase of the more civilized races.   It
does not follow as a matter of course that such a development means the movement of man to a desirable goal.
But (as Prof. Bury reminds us) Darwin, after pointing
to the fact that all the living forms of life are lineal
descendants of those which lived long before the Silurian
epoch, argues that we may look with some confidence
to a secure future of equally immeasurable length ;   and,
further, that, as natural selection works solely by and for
the good of each being, all corporeal and mental endow-
ments will tend to progress towards perfection.   Darwin
was a convinced optimist.

Equally so was Spencer.   According to him, change
is the law of all things, and man is no exception to it.
Humanity is indefinitely variable, and perfectibility is
possible.   All evil results from the non-adaptation of the

organism to its conditions.   In the present state of the
world men suffer many evils, and this shows that their
characters are not yet adjusted to the social state.   Now
the qualification requisite for the social state is that each
individual shall have such desires only as may fully be
satisfied without trenching upon the ability of others to
obtain similar satisfaction.   This qualification is not
yet fulfilled, because civilized man retains some of the
characteristics which were suitable for the conditions
of his earlier predatory life.   He needed one moral
constitution for his primitive state ; he requires quite
another for his present state.   The result is *a process of
adaptation* which has been going on for a long time, and
will go on for a long time to come.   Civilization repre-
sents the adaptations which have already been accomplished.   *Progress means the successive steps of the
process.*   (There we have the scientific definition of human
progress according to the apostle of evolution.)   The
ultimate development of the *ideal* man by this process
(says Spencer) is logically certain—as certain as any
conclusion in which we place the most implicit faith :
for instance, that men will all die.   Progress is thus held
by Spencer to be not an accident, but a necessity.   In
order that the human race should enjoy the greatest
amount of happiness, each member of the race should
possess   faculties   enabling   him   to   experience   the
highest   enjoyment   of   life,   yet   in   such   a   way   as
not to diminish the power of others to receive like
satisfaction.

Let me say, in order to avoid misapprehension, that
in what follows I am not citing Prof. Bury, but stating my
own opinions and suggestions.   It has been urged in
opposition to the optimistic doctrine of Darwin and
Spencer that it is a prominent fact of history that every

great civilization of the past progressed to a point at which, instead of advancing further, it stood still and declined. Arrest, decadence, decay, it is urged, have been the rule. This, however, is but the superficial view of the historian who limits his vision to the last four or five thousand years of man's development. It is not confirmed when we trace man from the flint-chippers of 500,000 years ago to the present day.

Naturalists are familiar with the phenomenon of *degeneration* in animal descent. Higher, more elaborate forms have sometimes given rise to simplified, dwindled lines of descent, specialized and suited to their peculiar environments. The frequent occurrence of such development in the direction of simplification and inferiority, and even the extinction of whole groups or branches of the genealogical tree of organisms, endowed with highly developed structural adaptations, and the survival of groups of extreme simplicity of structure, does not invalidate the truth of the conclusion as to a vast and predominating evolution—with increase of structure and capacity—of the whole stock of animal and vegetable organisms. A similar line of argument applies to the long and extended history of mankind.

The conclusion adverse to the reality of the evolutional progress of mankind which is held by those who declare that the ancient Greeks and other products of human evolution of like age had developed a degree of artistic execution and feeling, of devotion to intellectual veracity and ideal justice, to which more modern civilization has not attained, is a fanciful exaggeration in which it pleases some enthusiasts to indulge. [But an examination of the facts makes it abundantly clear that the conclusion is altogether erroneous.

Another attempt to discredit the belief in progress consists in an ambiguous use of the word " happiness " when it is declared that the teeming millions of China or even the herds of sheep browsing on our hill-sides are " happier " than the civilized peoples of Europe and America. Spencer's definition of the goal of human progress as determined by the general laws of organic evolution should lead in this discussion either to the abandonment of the use of the vague term " happiness," or to a critical examination of the state of feeling which it implies, and of the causes to which they are specifically related.

When we ask whether the conditions which have been the essential factors in human evolution and progress are still in operation and likely to operate for an indefinite period in the same direction, there is, it seems, in spite of the view as to their permanence held both by Spencer and by Darwin, room for doubt and for re-examination of the situation. The struggle for existence, the natural selection thereby of favoured variations, and their transmission by physical heredity from parent to offspring, suffice to explain the evolution of man's bodily structure from that of preceding ape-like animals, and even to account for the development of man's brain to greatly increased size and efficiency.

But a startling and most definite fact in this connection has to be considered and its significance appreciated. The fact to which I refer is that since prehistoric man, some hundred thousand years ago, attained the bodily structure which man to-day possesses, there has been no *further* development of that structure—measurable and of such quality as separates the animals nearest to man from one another. Yet man has shown enormous

" progress " since that remote epoch. The brain and the mental faculties connected with it have become the dominant and only progressive, " evolving," attribute of man.   Nevertheless, in regard to the brain there is, since the inception of the new phase of development which we have now to consider, no increase of size, though were we able to compare the ultimate microscopic structure of the brains of earlier and later man we should almost certainly find an increased complexity in the minute structure of the later brain.

It seems to be the fact that—when once man had acquired and developed the power of communicating and receiving thought, by speech with his fellow-man (so as to establish, as it were, mental co-operation), and yet further of recording all human thought for the common use of both present and future generations, by drawing and writing (to be followed by printing)—a totally new factor in human evolution came into operation of such overwhelming power and efficiency as to supersede entirely the action of natural selection of favoured bodily variations of structure in the struggle for existence. Language provided the mechanism of thought.   Recorded language — preserved and handed on from generation to generation as a thing external to man's body—became an ever-increasing gigantic heritage, independent of the mechanism of variation and of the survival of favoured variations which had hitherto determined the organic evolution of man as of his ancestry.   The observation, thought, and tradition of humanity, thus independently accumulated, continually revised, and extended, have given to later men that directing impulse which we call the moral sense, that still, small voice of conscience, the voice of his father-men, as well as that knowledge and skill which we call science and art. These things are, and have been, of far greater service to man in his struggles with the destructive forces of Nature and with competitors of his own race than has been his strength of limb and jaw. Yet they are not " inborn " in man. The young of mankind enter upon the world with a mind which is a blank sheet of " educable " quality, upon which, by the care of his elders or by the direction of his own effort, more or less of the long results of time embodied in the Great Record, the chief heritage of humanity, may be inscribed.

From this point of view it becomes clear that knowledge of " that which is," and primarily, knowledge of the Great Record, must be the most important factor in the future " Progress of Mankind." Thus one of the greatest services which man can render to his fellows is to add to the common heritage by making new knowledge of " that which is," whilst a no less important task is that of sifting truth from error, of establishing an unfailing devotion to veracity, and of promoting the prosperity of present and future generations of his race by facilitating, so far as lies within human power, the assimilation by all men of the chief treasures of human experience and thought.

The laws of this later " progress " are not, it would seem, those of man's earlier evolution. What they are, how this new progress is to be made more general and its continuance assured, what are the obstacles to it and how they are to be removed, are matters which have not yet been adequately studied. The infant science of psychology must eventually help us to a better understanding. Not only the reasoning intelligence, but also the driving power of emotion must be given due consideration. " Education " not only of the youth, but

6

also of the babe and of the adult, must become the all-commanding interest of the community. Progress will cease, to a large extent, to be a blindly attained outcome of natural selection ; it will acquire new characteristics as the conscious purpose of rational man.

CHAPTER IX

IS NATURE CRUEL ?

THE proposition that " Nature is cruel " is often discussed in an off-hand way and readily furnishes a text for the most divergent expressions of reason or of sentiment. The fact is that the fundamental difficulty of all human conceptions as to the origin and governance of the universe—namely, the existence of evil—is raised by it, whilst at the same time the terms " Nature " and " cruel " can be defined at will to mean as much or as little as the disputant may choose.

The book by my friend Mr. H. G. Wells, entitled " The Undying Fire," is a beautiful and fascinating parody of the great discussion between Job and his comforters. It is in many respects the finest of his efforts to bring home to all thoughtful men their possession of a deep-lying faith which, variously disguised by words and metaphors, they yet inevitably share as an indestructible inheritance from long ages of human struggle and victory. In Mr. Wells's book the staggering problem of " Cruelty in Nature " is trenchantly set forth. A ruined schoolmaster—the Job of the story—overwhelmed by financial and professional disaster, appalled by the horrors of the war which has taken his only son—tortured by a wretched wife—and now smitten by a deadly and painful disease—sets out, weary as he is, for a walk in the country, led on by visions of cool green shade and kindly streams beneath the trees and by desire for the fellowship of shy and gentle creatures.

But, instead of gaining rest and comfort, he is attacked by bloodthirsty gnats and flies, and the itching torture caused by those minute red beasts the "harvesters." A young rabbit, torn and bloody, lies in his path; the victims of a butcher-bird, spiked on thorns, wriggle on a hawthorn-bush. A villainous-looking cat drops a mangled young bird at his feet. Then for the rest of the day our Job can think of nothing but the feeble miseries of living things. He passes in review the constant panic, the savage sexual combats of the great beasts—the buffalo and the rhinoceros—the ceaseless prowling of the murderous but sickly tiger. Then he expatiates with scientific accuracy on the horrors of parasitic infection by worms, moulds, and bacteria, and finally reviews the reckless, destructive cruelty of profit-seeking man, who, in the remote Antarctic, driven by his insatiable greed, boils down penguins and whales for their fat and consigns their young to starvation without remorse, and in other regions burns and uproots forests, leaving arid deserts as the monuments of his activity. "Is this," he asks, "a world made for the happiness of sentient things? I ask you how is it possible for man to be other than a rebel in the face of such facts? . . . For these things are not in the nature of sudden creations and special judgments; they have been produced fearfully and wonderfully by a process of evolution as slow and deliberate as our own. How can man trust such a maker to treat him fairly? Why should we shut our eyes to things that stare us in the face? Either the world of life is the creation of a being inspired by a malignity at once filthy, petty, and enormous, or it displays a carelessness, an indifference, a disregard for justice. . . ."

I think we may without hesitation limit the word "cruelty" in any such discussion as this to the infliction of pain by a reasoning intelligent being on another sentient being (1) either with the intention of deriving pleasure from the contemplation of the evidences of suffering which he has produced, or (2) in pursuit of some end of his own in the attainment of which he is entirely disregardful of the pain he may cause to others or of the relative proportion which the possibly beneficent altruistic quality of the end he is pursuing bears to the amount of pain which he inflicts. We cannot admit for the purpose of this discussion the poetical use of the word "cruel," which applies to the mere occurrence of pain or the unintelligent agents of pain, such as storm, fire, claw, and tooth. The "cruel crawling foam, the cruel hungry foam" of Charles Kingsley's "Sands o' Dee" is a legitimate personification of the death-dealing waters—all the more so that it is a return to the mode of thought of primitive man —but we must not be led away by such poetical imagery from the real significance of the statement that Nature is cruel. Only an intelligent, reasoning being can be cruel.

Nature, if by that word we mean merely the winds, rocks, seas, and the unintelligent, unreasoning living things—plants and animals—which are known to us— cannot be "cruel." If we assert that this vast mechanism which we call "Nature" is cruel, we imply that it is the instrument of an intelligent, reasoning being to whom we attribute cruelty. There is no escape from that proposition, except by the assumption that the Creator is neither omnipotent nor omniscient, and cannot control what he has made.

Mankind has been very unwilling to admit that it is incapable of forming a satisfactory conception of the

Creator. Man has persisted in declaring not merely his capacity but his right and even his duty to create a Creator, and naturally has created one in his own image. The Creator has very generally been held to be a man-like being, differing from man in the fact that he is omnipotent and omniscient and " immaterial " in substance. At the same time man has revolted against the inevitable conclusion that the Creator is cruel, although in his earlier fancy that was a prominent feature of his conception.

By various devices he has tried to remove this defect from his conception of the Creator, whom he has made the object of his adoration and worship. He has (in past days) called into existence alongside of the Creator a second immaterial being, " Satan," to whom he assigned the part of author of all evil. Satan was, however, declared to be a " fallen angel," one of the Creator's works, and his introduction, therefore, though purifying, as it were, the character of the Creator, does not remove from that Being the authorship of cruelty and all other evils, unless he is no longer supposed to be either omni-potent or omniscient. " Manichæism " is the name of the ancient Persian religion (A.D. 270), which most fully taught this dual system—identifying the Evil One with Darkness and the Beneficent One with Light.

It is interesting to find that Mr. Job Huss, the suffer-ing schoolmaster of Mr. Wells's book, boldly accepts and finds comfort in the dual theory—the powers of Evil in the outer world on the one hand and the " undying fire," the " God in my heart," on the other. They are con-ceptions similar to the " Veiled Being " and the Invisible King of Mr. Wells's earlier work, and enable him to present a very noble picture of man's unquenchable

hope, his wavering but ever-returning courage, his indestructible faith in the ultimate triumph of right.

But others have attempted to face the difficulty—as,
for instance, did John Stuart Mill—by the admission that
if we believe in the existence of a beneficent Creator of
the universe we must suppose that he is not omnipotent,
or he would have avoided the creation of evil, or else
that he is not omniscient, and so is unable to foresee the
results of his creative activity.

Another and more modest solution of the difficulty
has always been present to the minds of thoughtful men,
including the writer of the Book of Job. What justifica-
tion (they would say) have we for creating a Creator in
our own image—with human standards of right and
wrong, with intentions, thoughts, conceptions which can
be comprehended by our small minds and expressed
by our inept words reflecting our paltry experiences ?
None. So far are we from knowing the ultimate conditions of existence that we must admit that possibly
what we call good cannot exist unless accompanied by
what we call evil—that possibly what we call well-being
and happiness is necessarily and inevitably conditioned
by pain.

It is true that man through the ages has shown, as
he has gradually developed, a determined opposition to
the pains and restrictions imposed upon him as upon
other animals by the play of natural forces. He has
under the schooling of pain acquired an ever-increasing
reasoning intelligence and that unique mysterious endow-
ment which we call " consciousness." From this point
of view he may be regarded as " Nature's rebel," ever-
more using his mental gifts in order to escape or to

mitigate or antagonize the pains and penalties to which
other living things—devoid of those gifts—have to submit.
I have written of his efforts as " Nature's Insurgent
Son " in the Romanes lecture delivered at Oxford in
1905, reprinted in my book " The Kingdom of Man."
Long ago the Greek poet, Sophocles, celebrated man's
skill and triumphs—in a chorus of the " Antigone "—
ending with the words :

> " Stratagem hath he for all that comes ! Never the future
> Finds him resourceless ! Grievous diseases he combats,
> Oft from their grip doth he free himself. Death alone, vainly,
> Vainly he seeks to escape ; 'gainst Death he is helpless."

But we may, perhaps, more justly regard man not as
Nature's rebel but rather as Nature's pupil.   The pains,
that which some would rashly call " the cruelty " of
Nature, are the very means—must we not believe the
only possible means ?—by which man's unique mental
quality, his undying fire, his conscience, his soul, has
been set a-growing and is henceforth kept creating the
tradition and records of the race, though the individual
passes away in the slumber of death.

The scene of animal suffering pictured by Job Huss
in " The Undying Fire " is exaggerated by the morbid
sensibility of that unfortunate man.   Whatever the
measure we assign to that suffering it must be recognized
as a part of the great process by which human life and
conscious happiness has been evolved from non-sentient
" primeval slime."   More than sixty years ago Mr.
Rowell, then curator of the Ashmolean Museum, greatly
interested the University of Oxford by his essay on " the
beneficent nature of pain."   He insisted on the fact that
the nerves, by the stimulation of which painful sensations
are produced, are so disposed on the animal body as to
protect it from injury and destruction—the shrinking or

evasive movements which follow their stimulation (often automatically) being such as to withdraw this or that limb or other part of the body from laceration, destructive pressure, burning, or other dangerous contact, or else to cause the animal to flee, to hide, to attack, or otherwise avoid hostile destructive agencies. Were it not for pain, he argued, and we may add its correlative fear, animals would knock themselves to pieces, blunder into every kind of destructive situation—and animals would speedily come to an end. Those who would maintain that this is a " cruel " ordering of life must hold either that an intelligent Creator, if not cruel, would have abstained altogether from creating life, or would have made it altogether insensible to pain, though reacting to protective stimuli. In default of this they must deny what I am inclined to maintain—namely, that the ultimate evolution from living matter of conscious, reasoning, progressive, adventurous man is in itself so great a good as to vastly outweigh the relatively small accompanying pain.

I have ventured to speak of the pain of animals and man as small compared with the splendour and beneficence which increasingly appertain to human life. I frankly accept the doctrine that, looking at life as a whole, present pain is the necessary step to abounding joy and contentment.

I recognize that the admission of pain to this place of toleration must be considered as a question of proportion. And it therefore becomes important that we should have —what is no easy matter—some definite apprehension, if possible some measure, of what we call pain. We only really know " pain " by feeling it ourselves. We infer that others—similar to ourselves in structure, habit, and expression—have under identical conditions identical

experience of pain.   We too readily regard the violence
of shrinking movement, cries, and efforts to escape as not
merely convincing evidence of pain, but as a *measure*
of its intensity.   Yet we are all familiar with facts which
show that such evidence is fallacious.   God forbid that
we should ever under-estimate or be indifferent to the
terrible suffering which many of our fellow-men have
experienced, and which others do now and will in the
future experience !   But we must at once accept as a
fact that pain is a mental condition which is not measurable either by the nature and severity of an injury or by
the cries and struggles which follow such injury.   We
know that a break in the great nerve complex, the spinal
cord, will result in loss of all sensation below the region of
injury, although violent movement (usually regarded as
indicative of pain) and shrinking from pain will continue.
We know that anæsthetics will arrest the consciousness
of pain and that what is called " the hypnotic condition " can be induced without the administration of any
drug and can be used for the same purpose.   We know
that strong, healthy men are much less sensitive to what
are usually pain-giving blows and injuries than are
more delicate, so-called " nervous " individuals.   The
Australian " savages " decorate their bodies by cutting
and scarring them without regard to pain, and the Poly-
nesians used to batter one another's skulls without serious
suffering—to an extent incomprehensible to Europeans.
Mere excitement or intense preoccupation often renders
men indifferent to—and even unaware of—injuries which,
in other circumstances, would be intensely painful.
Hence we must be cautious in measuring the pain even of
our fellow-men by the presumed pain-causing quality of
an injury or by the movements and cries which it excites.
Still more so is this the case when we endeavour to
estimate the pain endured by animals—other than man.

We have, then, reason to believe that pain is a protection to animals (including man in that category), an
automatic warning to avoid self-destruction and danger.
The lower animals—leaving aside for the moment the
warm-blooded mammals and birds—exhibit very definite
life-preserving mechanisms which act automatically
when danger or injury occurs, and, in many cases, have
been shown experimentally to be unassociated with a
condition identical with that of the " pain " of conscious
man.   We have no reason to suppose that the movements
of an injured earth-worm are in any way an expression or
measure of pain : they are vigorous efforts to remove or
escape from a life-threatening agency.   The great student
of insect life and behaviour—M. Fabre—states as his
conclusion that insects are marvellous automata and
that *ils ne savent rien de rien*.   We are not justified
in supposing that they feel pain.   We cannot admit
that Isabella (in " Measure for Measure ") is right when
she says :

> " The poor beetle, that we tread upon,
>   In corporal sufferance finds a pang as great
>   As when a giant dies."

What she says just before—namely, that " the sense of
death is most in apprehension," is, on the other hand,
profoundly true in regard to man, though probably
not in regard to any animals, and it is also true of man
if we substitute for " sense of death " the " sense of
pain."   Thus we are led to conclude that the slaughtered
rabbit, the butcher-bird's larder, the fluttering bird
dropped by the cat, and the vast array of parasites cited
by Mr. Job Huss are not evidences of a vast amount
of suffering comparable to that which a conscious,
reflecting human being might experience were he the
victim.   We are not warranted in supposing that even
he would necessarily suffer to the extent which imagina-

tion and sympathy suggest. It is very doubtful whether the higher animals hunted and wounded by man and by carnivorous animals, or fighting with one another, experience much pain. Their excitement inhibits pain, as we learn from men who have escaped after having been mauled and carried off by a lion. It appears certain that such highly organized creatures as fish have no prolonged suffering as the result of injury, though probably a " pang " is experienced by them, sufficient to turn them *momentarily* from a dangerous situation. A fish has been caught by a hook on which its own eye had been accidentally impaled and torn from its head. It was greedily " taken " by the fish as a bait.

I know how disagreeable a subject this is, and how readily one can be misunderstood and misjudged when one attempts to state the truth about it. But one striking illustration of the fact that shrinking, and what often passes for evidence of great pain, may be a misinterpretation of automatic protective movements is afforded by the less shocking instance of the sensitive plant (Mimosa). When a leaflet of this plant is pinched, it and its neighbouring leaflets quickly droop, one by one. If the leaf-stem is struck the whole group of pinnate leaves close down and the stem bends quickly and deeply as though in acute pain and fear. Yet this is only the result of the movement of liquid within certain tracts of tissue in the plant serving it as a protection against assault. After a few minutes the stems rise again and the leaflets expand in neatly ordered rows. We are surely not justified in supposing that the sensitive plant suffers what we human creatures call " pain." It is certain that a vast number of lower animals are as incapable of feeling pain as is the sensitive plant. Even the highest animals are far less liable to continued pain than are civilized men

A word seems necessary as to the attribution of cruelty to the cat when " playing " with an injured mouse. The cat, not being a reasoning conscious being, is incapable of cruelty. Its behaviour is automatic, as also is that of the mouse. The cat takes no pleasure in the signs of suffering as such, shown by the mouse, and if it could or did do so, it would misinterpret the movements of the mouse, which are not accompanied by pain any more, or very little more, than is the jumping of a ball of paper pulled by a string.

Thus we are led to the judgment that the supposition that there is an immense amount of needless pain going on in the world is a misinterpretation of the facts. There *is* pain, but it is mostly short and sharp and of a directive and protective character. Man has been, and is still being, educated by pain. He has to a large extent gained control of it or learnt to avoid it—in so far as he is himself concerned—but there is still a gigantic task in this connection before him. He has not yet put an end to war, famine, and disease. It seems that this strange and directive thing—the liability to pain—increases and appears in unforeseen ways, as man becomes more developed. Education and the great tradition—the record of humanity, the creator of his soul and its " undying flame "—whilst they have enabled him to avoid many causes of pain—are building up new ones for him. An endless variety of " things "—experiences, actions, relations which were to him matters of indifference— have now become active sources of either pleasure or of pain. A large and important branch of the attempt to understand the history and origin of pain is indicated by this consideration, but I cannot now pursue it.

The main tendency of what I have said leads to the

conclusion that pain is not, in the great scheme of the universe, " cruel," but the beneficent guide of the development of sentient beings. Man's sense of justice leads him to condemn the infliction of even the smallest amount of pain on man by his fellow-man, for however good a purpose, without the assent of the sufferer. Still more does he resent the conclusion of his own life (to the inception of which he has not been a consenting party) by inevitable and arbitrary death. But he does not " curse God and die," a course which is freely open to him. On the contrary, he clings to his life and its more or less painful incidents for the sake of the pleasure which he derives from his own adventurous existence and from sympathy with that of his race. He continually and necessarily balances " pain " against " well-being " and voluntarily submits himself and others to a present but transient pain in order to gain the larger well-being and happiness—not of himself alone but of future men.

Similarly, he finds that every moment of his life is dependent on the destruction and unconsenting painful experience—evanescent as it is—of a host of lower animals and of plants. He does not act in consequence according to the formal rules of an impossible and visionary justice : he deliberately balances the good against the evil. In proportion as he is reasonable and intelligent he uses his weaker living companions with such moderation and mercy as are consistent with the continued development of the life and soul of man. In so doing he is consciously or unconsciously striving to adjust his aims and his actions to the " one increasing purpose "—Great Nature's unfolding—which has brought him from the womb of time to his present estate.

CHAPTER X

THE SENSES AND SENSE-ORGANS

IN the skin and underlying the surfaces of deep-lying organs inside the body there is an enormous number of microscopically small root-like fibrils or filaments of extreme tenuity penetrating in every direction. They are the finest nerve filaments, threads, or fibres. They gather together into skeins or " strands," and these again into larger bundles called " nerves," and thus pass from the surface and other parts of the body where they commence, joining to form larger and larger bundles until they reach the brain, either entering it directly or by way of the great spinal cord, which lies in the bony colonnade formed by the backbone or vertebral column. There are nerve-fibres, the business of which is to bring " impulses "—as it were, wordless messages—from the body and its surface *to* the brain and spinal cord. They are called " afferent " fibres. And there are other nerve-fibres, undistinguishable in appearance from these, and often mixed in with them in one bundle or nerve, whose business it is to convey impulses or wordless messages *from* the brain and spinal cord to muscles and gland-cells. They are called " efferent " fibres. The rate of passage of these impulses has been measured. They travel at the rate of 400 feet per second.

In this chapter we are concerned with the afferent

nerve-fibres. They are often called "sensory nerve-fibres," whilst the efferent ones are called "motor nerve-fibres." The endings or beginnings of the finest afferent nerve-fibres or threads near the surface of the body or of its internal cavities are of such a nature that the nerve-fibres can be acted upon by various external agencies, such as pressure, change of temperature, light, chemical and electrical disturbance ; that is to say, the "state" or condition of the living nerve-fibre can be definitely altered by the impact of these agencies. The action of these agencies on the nerve-fibres is spoken of as the "stimulation" or "excitation" of the nerve-fibre. The immediate fact by which this "stimulation" is made evident is the setting up of rapid changes, both chemical and electrical, in the substance of the nerve-fibre. These rapid changes are called "impulses" or "nerve-impulses," and are transmitted or propagated along a nerve-fibre with a quickness of 400 feet a second—which is less than but resembles that of an electric current—until they reach the nerve-cell to which it belongs, one of millions contained in the brain and spinal cord. The nerve-cell is a plump, granular lump of protoplasmic substance, with a large spherical kernel or nucleus, and with many branching fibrils reaching out from its substance and joining it to other nerve-cells. The nerve-cells with which we are here concerned are those which exist by millions in the brain, and form what is called "the grey substance of the brain." Arrived here the impulse, or a whole series of such impulses coming to many brain-cells, produces further changes, which give rise to those mental conditions which we call "sensations." I do not propose, at this moment, to go further into the relation of the structure of the brain to mental activities ; but I will say—what is the unshaken and unanimous conviction of all physiologists—namely, that it is by " sensations," and only by sensations, that we arrive at knowledge of the world around us and of our own bodies.

In order that external agencies may thus act on the fine terminal twigs of the nerves it is necessary that the endings of these delicate filaments be connected with a receptive apparatus, an " end-organ," as it is termed, which is adapted to receive the special action of one or other of the external agencies I have named above, and so set up the stimulation of the fine nerve-threads which end in it. There is one kind of end-organ which is specially fitted to the action of light—or, as we say, is specially " sensitive " to light; another kind which is specially sensitive to the vibrations of sound; another which is so for the chemical actions causing taste; another for those causing smell; another for those set up by mechanical pressure; another for rise of temperature (heat); another for fall of temperature (cold); another for the changes of pressure in liquid-holding tubes caused by alterations of balance and equilibrium; another for the muscular contractions which enable us to estimate weight; and another for those violent and destructive changes in our tissues which cause the sensation which we call " pain." There thus appear to be some ten distinct groups of sensations, requiring and associated with distinct end-organs connected with special nerve-fibres and specially fitted to receive the stimulating influence of ten different kinds of actions or changes which occur as we live and move in relation to other existing things and as they move and change around us.

The more or less elaborate mechanisms formed at the free ends of sensory nerves are called " sense-organs." The special capacity and working of a sense-organ is called a " sense." Thus there are ten " senses," each of a different kind, appropriate each to one of the ten different kinds of sense-organs. The four first mentioned in my list above given are often called " special senses," and their end-organs are called the organs of special sense. They are : (1) sight, (2) hearing, (3) smell, and (4) taste. The organs of these senses are separate parts, distinctly and easily recognized, and in the case of the first two greatly elaborated and brought to perfection by obvious " accessory " apparatus, which assists or helps to render the sense-organ responsive to small quantities of the stimulating agent and to other features connected with it, such as the direction from which it comes and the variation (often very great) in its special qualities.

Thus we have the eye (a pair or more in different animals), which consists not merely of the light-sensitive retina, built up by most peculiar end-cells (the retinal-cells), in which the nerve-threads of the optic nerve terminate, but of the eyeball, provided with lenses, which can be " focused " so as to produce a picture in its dark chamber, where the retina or sensitive plate is spread, also provided with the series of muscles under nerve-control which turn the axis of the eyeball in different directions, and the circular curtain of the iris and also the eyelids by which the amount of light entering the eyeball can be regulated. There are also minute elaborations of great importance in the retinal-cells, such as those connected with the discrimination of colours.

The second organ of " special sense," the ear (usually, as in man, a pair), is less obvious than the eye. For what we commonly call " the ear " is only an external " hearing trumpet," the real organ of hearing being sunk in the bones of the skull and called " the internal ear."

It is an elaborately constructed membranous sac, containing liquid. It is of the shape of a coiled snail-shell, with three loop-like tubes—-the semicircular canals—growing out of it. On its walls are distributed an immense profusion of bunches of fine nerves, which gather together to constitute the auditory nerve. The ends of these fine nerves penetrate the wall of the snail-shaped sac, and are connected with peculiar end-cells and hair-like rods, forming in its inside a complex apparatus, of which different elements are excited by the vibrations of notes of different pitch, resulting in a difference of sensation for all the immense variety of sounds and musical combinations which assail it in the form of sound-vibrations.

The organ of the sense of smell is placed on the passage by which air enters the lungs—the nasal passage—and the nerve-threads of the two olfactory nerves, which pass directly from it to the brain, end (or, to put it the other way, originate) in the nasal cavity in a multitude of rod-like cells, which cover the walls of the much-folded and deep recesses into which ultra-microscopic odoriferous particles or gases are carried by the inspired air. The perfection of this sense-organ consists in its sensibility to extremely minute quantities of odoriferous matter, and its property of being differently affected by odoriferous particles which differ only in the minutest degree, chemically, from one another. Thus the dog is differently affected by the odoriferous particles given off by different human beings, and can thus recognize an individual, or even his mere footprints, by his smell, a power which, to judge by the size and structure of his nasal cavities, man also, in some remote period, possessed, but has (with some rare exceptions) now lost.

The sense-organs of taste are found in the tongue : they, like the organ of smell, are not so complex as the organs of sight and hearing, but are limited to furnishing a different sensation according to the chemical composition of substances presented to them. The substances which can be " tasted " must be soluble in water, and the different sensations which they produce are only distinguishable by us as sweet, bitter, sour, and salt, of greater or less intensity. Very usually people call by the name " taste " what is really due to the sense of smell. All " flavours " of foods and drinks are really odours which reach the olfactory organs from substances held in the mouth. The end-organs of the nerve of taste are little bulb-like groups of cells which are set on tuft-like projections of the tongue or in circular grooves far back on its surface. Bitter and sweet taste are dependent on end-organs distinct from those which are concerned with acid and salt taste, and there seem also to be separate end-bulbs for sweet taste distinct from those for bitter taste. The nerve-fibres connected with the taste-organs do not unite to form a pure nerve of taste. The optic nerve is formed purely by nerves from the retina, the auditory nerve purely by nerves from the auditory sac, and the olfactory nerve purely by nerves from the olfactory recesses of the nasal cavity. But the taste nerve-fibres pass to the brain in the glossopharyngeal nerve, and also in the lingual branch of the fifth nerve in company with fibres of other kinds. In this respect the sense of taste resembles the less elaborated senses, namely, those of touch, heat, cold, the muscular sense, the sense of pain, and apparently also the sense of equilibrial pressure, which though not concerned with sound-vibrations is conveyed to the brain by fibres which form part of the auditory nerve.

These less elaborated and less specialized " senses "

have until recent years been classed vaguely with the
sense of touch, and the term " general sensibility " has
also been used so as to include them.   Thus, it was usual
to speak of the five senses, or five gateways of knowledge
—sight, hearing, smell, taste, and touch.   But, really,
it seems that there is a distinct apparatus and distinct
nerve-threads, and a distinct sensation, for (1) the sense
of heat, (2) the sense of cold, (3) the muscular sense,
(4) the equilibrial sense, (5) the sense of pain, as well as
for (6) the sense of touch.   So that we recognize ten
distinct senses.   The nerve-fibres of the sense of touch
are distributed in the skin all over the body, and pass by
nerve-bundles, containing other kinds of nerves, to the
spinal cord and brain.   The same is true of the sense of
heat, the sense of cold, the muscular sense, and the sense
of pain, with some qualification as to the precise regions
of the body thus provided.   The nerves appear to end in
or between the surface-cells of the skin in the first two, and
in the muscular cells in the third.   The sense of pain is
excited by the stimulation of nerves (in many, but not
all, parts of the body), by destructive processes, such as
cutting or crushing, and also especially by the condition
called inflammation.   It is probable that only special
nerve-fibres are capable of being stimulated so as to
produce the sensation of pain.

It has been shown experimentally that the sensation
caused by contact of the skin of the hand or other part with
a surface which is quickly *raised* in temperature, or, as we
say, " warmed," may be brought about in a person who
has, by disease or injury, lost the sense of cold in that
part, that is to say, is unable to recognize a sudden *fall* in
the temperature to which it is exposed, and that a fall of
temperature in other cases is recognized where rise of
temperature produces no sensation.   Hence it is inferred

that there are separate nerve-fibres and nerve-end-organs concerned in the heat-sense and the cold-sense.

On the other hand, in many parts of the surface of the body the sense of touch is more acutely developed than it is in others, and there we find special end-organs called tactile-bulbs. These are minute spherical or oblong groups of compressed cells in which the terminations of nerve-fibres are enclosed. They are particularly abundant in the fine ridges separated from one another by grooves, which mark the finger-tips with whorls and loop-like patterns. The sense of touch is the sense of slight mechanical pressure—rough and smooth surfaces causing difference of pressure when the finger, or whatever part of the body is used as the exploring instrument, is moved over such surface in contact with it. Great tactile discrimination is thus possible, and we see the extent to which it can be carried by the wonderful skill obtained by the blind, who can not only read " by touch " the embossed printing of the Braille books prepared for them, but can distinguish and recognize a great variety of surfaces of different kinds, which ordinary men who are not dependent on their sense of touch, and so have not cultivated it, cannot distinguish in that way. The sense of touch is variously developed on regions of the body other than the finger-tips, as may be shown by the distance between two points of pressure (such as the tips of a pair of compasses) required in order that their existence as separate points of touch may be recognized. Points, where nerve-fibres capable of stimulation by touch exist, are surrounded by larger or smaller insensible areas. The points of sensibility are less closely set in the less sensitive regions of the body surface.

With regard to the muscular sense, it seems that the

cells of the muscular tissue may be the end-organ of the sensory nerves. Such end-organs certainly exist and enable us to estimate " weight " by the amount of muscular effort necessary to hold up a given body and prevent it from falling to the ground.

The sense of equilibrium has its sense-organ in the three semicircular canals of the internal ear. These are membranous tubes filled with liquid and lying in liquid. They are set in the three planes of a cube. A new movement in any plane or the sudden cessation of previous movement in any plane will cause more or less of what is ordinarily called a " jerk " or " chuck " in the liquid-holding membranous tube, and as the three ultimate planes of space of three dimensions are represented by three corresponding semicircular tubes each will be affected according to the direction of the movement, and a corresponding pressure on the end-organs of the nerves distributed to its walls will result. Since there is a set of these canals in the inner ear on each side of the head, the apparatus furnishes the necessary nerve-impulses and sensations for a comparison of the relation of the two sides of the head to any movement, and consequently a resultant sensation which is indicative of the equilibrium and poise of the head and of the direction of movement. Birds in which one of the canals is injured cannot fly ; they cannot " feel " their balance or want of balance and adapt the movement of the wings accordingly. Rats and rabbits so injured cannot walk straight. When the canals of the internal ear of one side are diseased in man giddiness and a tendency to fall in the attempt to walk are consequences. The pair of liquid-holding vesicles containing one or more solid particles suspended within them, which are found in snails, mussels, and other molluscs, are usually called " internal ears " or " auditory vesicles," because they are affected by the vibrations of sound. But it has been reasonably contended that they must serve if not exclusively, yet also as organs of the sense of balance—and hence in place of the name " otocysts " or " ear-vesicles " they have been called " statocysts " or " balance vesicles." The walls of these sacs in the lower animals are supplied each by a large nerve from the brain, the fine fibres of which end in peculiar " cells " which line the vesicle. A few years ago similar vesicles were discovered in the leaves of plants, especially in those which climb and twist round the stems of other plants for support. It appears that they may serve as directive organs in the movements of these plants, though such a notion involves the supposition that the living protoplasm of plant tissues can act as the nervous system does in animals and transmit " impulses." Mr. Darwin did not shrink from such a supposition, and in his last work—that on the movement of plants—he established the existence of such " transmission " in several cases.

By this brief review I have placed before the reader an outline of what is meant by a " sense." It is always dependent on the excitation of a demonstrable and appropriate apparatus—a sense-organ—and through it of connected nerve-fibres, which transmit " impulses " to the brain. We have seen what are the agencies which can be distinguished as definitely stimulating nerve-fibres in this way, and that there are ten different kinds of such agencies acting on ten differently constructed appropriate sense-organs (some few of them not yet fully investigated), in which the nerves terminate, or perhaps we should rather say " take origin." In view of these facts, the absurdity of talking about " a sixth-sense " (there are already ten), or a " spider-sense," or a " cat-sense," becomes obvious. It is, of course, conceivable and possible that a spider or a cat may act with some unusual intensity in some people on one of the ten " senses " which have been distinguished by investigators of the human nervous system. But we must require experimental demonstration of the fact before accepting assertions on the subject, whilst those who invoke a new special " sense " to bolster up their untested beliefs in the stories of detection of concealed spiders and cats must, it seems, be using the word " sense " in a misleading and illegitimate manner.

So, too, it seems to me that there is a fundamental misunderstanding as to the nature and operation of the only channels by which man is known to receive impressions, and those highly complicated groups of impressions which result in knowledge of the world around him—on the part of those who are of the opinion that one human brain can communicate, not merely signs, but detailed information to another at a distance without operating on the sense-organs of the recipient. I refer to the baseless assertions of the existence of what has been called " telepathy."

CHAPTER XI

AN EYE AT THE BACK OF THE HEAD

I MAGINATIVE people have been heard to excuse a failure to keep in view everything going on around them—back and front, right and left—by the protest: " How could I possibly see it ? I haven't got eyes at the back of my head ! " " True, Madam (or Sir)," we should reply ; " yet the notion is not so outlandish as you seem to suppose. Those graceful, swiftly evasive little animals, the lizards, closely similar in all details of structure to ourselves, have, besides a pair of eyes like our own, also a single eye in the middle of the top of the head ! "

This third eye is, it is true, of small size, and was only discovered a few years ago. But it is a true " eye," an optical apparatus like a minute photographic camera with lens, dark chamber and a sensitive nerve-plate corresponding to the photographer's sensitive plate, and connected by a long, optic nerve with the brain. It is only in the lizards, among living reptiles, that this third eye is to-day existing, but in some of the ancient, extinct reptiles it was of large size and great importance. The common little green lizard of Jersey and South Europe shows it very well, though it is larger in the large tropical lizards known as " Monitors," and in the curious Sphenodon or " Tua-tara " of New Zealand.

Fig. 24 is a drawing of the upper surface of the head of the green lizard, of twice the natural length and breadth. It is covered by horny plate or " scales " arranged in a definite pattern. The nostrils perforate a pair of these " scales." That of the right side is marked *n.* in our drawing. Farther back we come to the large paired

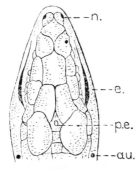

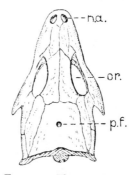

FIG. 24.—Upper surface of the head of the Green Lizard, Lacerta viridis, magnified to twice the natural length. *n.*, right nostril; *e.*, eyelid of the large eye of the right side; *au.*, auditory canal; *p.e.*, scale covering the pineal, or " third " eye, which occupies the parietal foramen.

FIG. 25.—The upper surface of the bony skull of the same Lizard. *n.a.*, the right nasal aperture; *or.*, the right orbit; *p.f.*, the parietal foramen, or orifice, in which the " third " eye is seated.

eyes, which, seen from above, show only as two dark slits edged by the eyelids. That of the right side is marked *e.* Still farther back there is a pair of small openings of which that on the right side is marked *au.* They are the ear passages. In the middle line is a five-sided scale marked *p.e.*, with a little translucent prominence at its centre. This is the special thing which concerns us ; it is the covering scale of " the third eye," and seems to be shaped so as to act as a window or look-out for that remarkable possession.

When the scales and soft parts are cleaned off the head of the green lizard, the bony skull is displayed as drawn in our Fig. 25. The cavities in the bone connected with the outer nostrils are seen (*n.a.*) and the bony orbits (*or.*) in which the large " eyeballs " or paired eyes are supported and protected. In the middle line of the big bone, called the " parietal," which is the roof of the chamber containing the lizard's brain, there is a small round hole (*p.f.*). This is the " parietal foramen," or opening. It corresponds exactly in position with the scale marked *p.e.* in Fig. 24. Filling this parietal aperture, when the soft parts are still in place, lies a little dark-coloured globe about as big as a small pin's head. This is the actual thing of which we are in search—the third eye itself. The little ball-like, grey-coloured homœopathic globule has a stalk attached to it—its optic nerve—which passes through the hole in the bone and between the lobes of the enclosed brain to join the deeply placed central part of that organ.

If we carefully expose the globule-like object of our search in its place by cutting away the skin and soft parts on one side, and examine it with a magnifying glass, it presents the appearance shown in Fig. 26, with half of the overlying scale in position (Fig. 26, *cut.*). The horny cuticle (*cut.*) of the scale and the underlying layer of epidermis (*ep.*) are seen in section, whilst the " eye " itself is uncut and supported on its nerve-stalk (*n.s.*). The surface of the ball of the little eye is seen to be beset with black pigment threads excepting the part nearest the scale, which is colourless and transparent. [This is the " lens," so lettered in our figure. By skilful methods thin sections can be cut right through the eyeball and its stalk—for examination with high powers of the microscope. Such a section is drawn in Fig. 27, and the complete structure of the little " third eye " is revealed. It is hollow, the central space being filled by clear liquid. Its wall is built up of the microscopic units of structure known as " cells." In front they are massed so as to form the important firm and definitely shaped lens. It

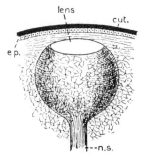

FIG. 26.—The " third " eye, or pineal eye, of the Green Lizard, exposed by dissection. *cut.*, cuticle ; *ep.*, cellular epiderm ; *lens*, the lens forming the top of the eyeball ; *n.s.*, the nerve stalk, or optic nerve.

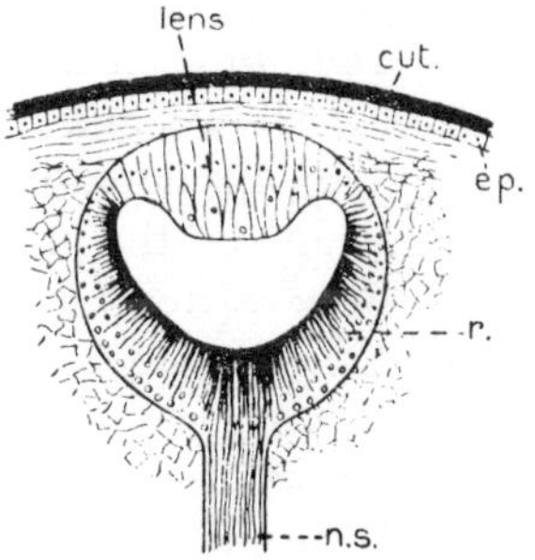

FIG. 27.—The same as Fig. 26, but the eyeball and its stalk now shown in section. *r.*, the retina lining the eyeball. Other letters as in Fig. 26. Note the cell-structure of the lens.

is a matter of significance that this lens is built up of interlocking living " cells," each with its little central sphere or " nucleus," and is not a structureless knob of horny substance or of dense jelly, as is the case with the lens of the eyes of some lower animals (see next chapter). The sides and back part of the wall of the chamber or cavity of the lizard's third eye is formed by two sets of interlocking rod-like cells (Fig. 27, *r.*), one set charged with black pigment, which thus give a dark, black lining to the chamber—a feature universally characteristic of true " eyes "—and the other set standing between these and connected each with a nerve-filament which can be traced with its fellows to the nerve-stalk (*n.s.*) built up of these filaments and passing as a long cord far down into the central part of the brain.

The little " third " eye we have thus examined is often called " the parietal eye," because it is lodged in an opening or " foramen " in the parietal bone—a bone formed by the union of a pair of bones which roof over the skull in ourselves and other vertebrate animals, such as fish, reptiles, birds, and mammals. The parietal eye is also often called " the pineal eye," because in ourselves and most other vertebrate animals it has dwindled and disappeared, leaving only a deep part of its stalk which is connected with the brain and with a pea-like body, called by old anatomists the " pineal body." The significance of the pineal body is unknown. It is not the parietal eye in an altered condition, and it is not yet possible to give any satisfactory account of it. The philosopher Descartes held it to be the seat of the soul. This part of the brain and the parietal eye itself are relics of the past—structures which either persist and are inherited from our remote ancestors in a changed and puzzling condition, or else have ceased to appear—even with changed shape and uses—in the present representatives of the vertebrate stock save in a very few exceptional instances. The only other living creatures, besides some lizards, in which the third or parietal or pineal eye has been found are the very peculiar and remote group of fish-like creatures known as lampreys and hag-fish—and in them its structure is less developed and its significance less obvious than in the lizards. It seems that the little parietal eye of the lizards is only a last vestige or survival of what was once a large and important third eye

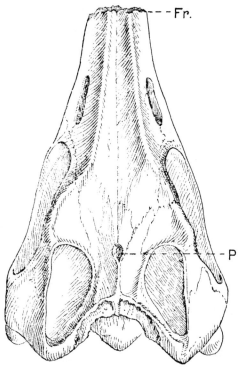

FIG. 28.—Dorsal surface of the skull of an Ichthyosaurus, to show P., the parietal orifice in which the pineal eye was lodged. Fr., the broken edge of the snout. (From a specimen in the Natural History Museum, reduced to one-fourth of the natural size.)

In many kinds of lizards the parietal eye is present, but in a withered, ineffective condition. Even in those in which it retains the window-scale, the lens, and the other details of structure as above described in the green lizard, it has not been shown to be actually in use as an organ of vision.   More experiments to test this are needed, and are not easy to carry out.   Possibly it has in all living lizards become so reduced in size as to be useless ; but possibly it still is sensitive to light in a small way. On the other hand, the skulls of some of the large, extinct reptiles—but not those of crocodiles, Dinosaurs, or tortoises—have a " parietal foramen " of an inch or more in diameter, and the " third eye," which was lodged in this orifice, must have been an important organ of sight. The skull of the extinct porpoise-like reptile, the Ichthyosaurus, has a large parietal foramen (Fig. 28) ; and the skulls of the Dicynodonts, huge tusk-bearing reptiles found in the pre-oolitic strata known as the Trias, possess a parietal foramen as big round as a penny, its bony edge raised up to form a sort of circular well-head.

It is not improbable that the well-grown parietal eye of the great extinct reptilian ancestors of our modern lizards was not only actually larger but more elaborately constructed than the diminutive parietal eye which I have described and pictured above

CHAPTER XII

OTHER EYES

EYES as simple as the lizard's parietal or third eye—described in Chapter XI—are characteristic of various kinds of lower animals, but are formed independently in different groups by the modification of parts essentially different in origin in each group. Thus in the scorpion and some other hard-skinned insects and insect-like creatures, we find a very simple kind of eye formed by a tubercle or knob of the hard covering of " chitin " or " cuticle " of the head (Fig. 29). From three to seven or more of these little eyes are found on each side of the scorpion's head. The living " cells " of the epidermis,

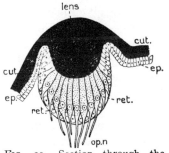

FIG. 29.—Section through the lateral eye of a Scorpion. *lens*, the lens formed by chitinous cuticle; *cut.*, the cuticle or outer layer of the skin; *ep.*, the cellular epidermis which secretes or deposits the horny cuticle and the lens; *ret.*, the nerve-end cells of the retina, which are part of the epidermic layer of cells; *op.n.*, the optic nerve fibres. (From the author's original drawing.)

which are sunk so as to form a shallow cup, not only secrete the nearly spherical lens of horny substance (which for emphasis is shown as black in our drawing,

8

though it is really clear and transparent), but are actually elongated beneath the lens and serve as the nerve-end cells, or " retinal " cells, to which the nerve-filaments of the optic nerve are attached.   In life, a black pigment is formed on the sides of each nerve-end cell, but has been dissolved by weak nitric acid in the microscopical section here drawn, since, if present, it would conceal the cells from view.   The important points about this simple " lateral eye " of the scorpion's head are, first, that the lens is not like that of the lizard's parietal eye, composed of " cells " forming the front wall of an eye vesicle or chamber, but is a button or knob of the outer horny, or " chitinous," cuticle ; and, second, that it is supported by —and is the secretion or product of—a single layer of enlarged cells, which not only give rise to this horny substance, but are, at the same time, the " retinal " or nerve-end cells—" the sensitive plate " upon which the light, concentrated by the lens, acts so as to produce " vision."   The " compound " eyes of insects and crus-taceans consist of many hundreds of closely packed little eyes, each essentially like one of the scorpion's simple eyes, but further elaborated in the structure and grouping of the soft living cells underlying each minute lens.

The paired eyes which both marine and terrestrial snails carry on their heads are, again, of a different make. The simplest—as, for instance, in the limpet—are open cups sunk in the skin, and filled with a transparent, structureless secretion, which is the lens (Fig. 30).   But in other snails the cup closes up in front and becomes a little sphere enclosing the glass-like lens (Fig. 31).   The back wall and sides of the cup (even in those cases where the cup is open) develop black pigment.   Embedded in this black pigment are nerve-end cells connected by the optic nerve with the brain (see Figs. 30 and 31, *pg.*).

The cuttle-fishes are elaborated and more highly developed snails adapted to a swimming life. Their paired eyes are in appearance (colour and shape) wonderfully like those of the true " fishes " and other vertebrates, but are really unlike them in growth and origin, and are actually elaborations of the

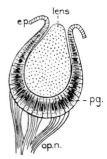

FIG. 30.— Section through the open cup-like eye of the Limpet. *lens*, the viscid plug of the eye " cup " acting as a lens ; *ep.*, the epidermis ; *pg.*, the pigment layer of the retina ; *op.n.*, the optic nerve.

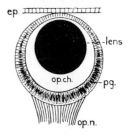

FIG. 31.—Section through the closed spherical eye of a Land-Snail. *ep.*, the epidermis from which the optic chamber (*op.ch.*) has become separated as a closed sphere ; *lens*, the spherical lens not completely filling the optic chamber (*op.ch.*) ; *pg.*, the pigment-layer of the retina ; *op.n.*, the optic nerve.

simpler eye of the snails. By up-growths a con tractile, perforated screen of metallic lustre, like the iris and " pupil " of the vertebrate's paired eye, is formed in the cuttle-fish in front of the closed cup containing the lens (see Fig. 32 and explanation) ; and a further and later transparent up-growth—the " cornea "—in front of this "iris" forms an " anterior chamber " to the eye, with clear, transparent walls, *a.ch.* The lens, which becomes firm and separate from the more fluid contents of the original

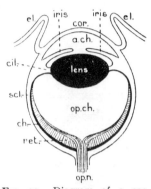

FIG. 32.—Diagram of a section through a highly developed eye representing that either of a Vertebrate or of a Cephalopod Cuttle-Fish. It shows anterior (*a.ch.*) and posterior chambers (*op.ch.*), an iris or adjustable curtain in front of the lens (marked *iris*), a "ciliary" muscle (*cil.*) which corrects the focus of the lens, and a strongly developed black pigment lining, the "choroid" coat of the eyeball (*ch.*) backing the retina (*ret.*); also the cornea (*cor.*) or transparent part of the wall of the eyeball; *scl.*, the tough opaque coat of the eyeball; and *el.*, the eyelids.

" eye-chamber," is now h ing up, as it were, between that chamber (which is now the posterior chamber) and the newly formed anterior chamber. A muscle—like in position to the " ciliary " muscle of the vertebrate's paired eye —is attached all round to the edge of the spherical lens (*cil.* in Fig. 32), and serves to move it a little so as to focus the picture made by the lens on the back wall of the posterior chamber, where is spread the much-elaborated sensitive plate of pigment and nerve-end cells called the " retina." A pair of movable eyelids grow up in the cuttle-fish, externally from the sides of the transparent wall of the anterior chamber—the cornea (*el.* in Fig. 32).

As though expressly to show us the real nature of the cuttle-fish's eye, we find in the Pearly Nautilus—a living though very anciently evolved relative of the cuttle-fishes—a pair of eyes each as large as a marrowfat pea, but of absolutely primitive construction. Each stands up like a kettledrum in shape,

opaque and dull-coloured (Fig. 33). But in the centre
of the flat surface of the drum is a minute hole giving
access to its black-lined cavity.
The sea-water has free access
by this little hole to the cavity,
and so have the rays of light
which, entering here, form a
picture on the black, sensitive,
retina-lined wall of the little
kettledrum. There is no
" lens " or other accessory
structure. Its simple structure
is shown by a section through it
(Fig. 33). It is what is called
a " pin-hole camera," and the
picture is produced within it
in virtue of the same optical
laws as were made use of in
the " camera obscura " shown
in bygone times at fairs and
seaside piers and pleasure-
gardens. I say " were," for
they seem to have gone out
of fashion. I have never had
the chance of coming across
this popular " show," though
I lately read a novel in which
the conversion of a cellar into
a " camera obscura " by the
accidental opening of a small
hole in its roof is made the
means whereby an unfortu-
nate artist finds himself an unwilling witness of a
murder going on, on the roof overhead—the whole scene
being projected as a picture on to the wall of the cellar,

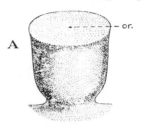

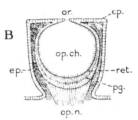

FIG. 33.—Eye of the Pearly
Nautilus.

A, the eyeball standing
up like a kettledrum—
seen from the surface;
or., the minute pin-hole
aperture by which the
light enters the eyeball.

B, diagram of a section
through the same; *or.*,
the pin-hole aperture, or
orifice; *op.ch.*, the optic
chamber lined with vibrating hairs (*cilia*); *ret.*,
the retina continuous
with the epidermis of the
outer surface; *pg.*, the
layer of pigment in the
retina; *op.n.*, the optic
nerve fibres converging
to form the optic nerve.

CHAPTER XIII

THE PAIRED EYES OF MAN

WE now come to the paired eyes of vertebrates, which, as just pointed out, have much the same elaboration of details and parts as we find in the cuttle-fish, and are equally well represented in a diagrammatic way by the section drawn in Fig. 32. We have the lens slung between an anterior and posterior chamber ; a transparent " cornea " forming the front wall of the anterior chamber ; the lens brought to focus by the action of a special " ciliary " muscle, and overhung in front by a circular muscle—the iris—which can expand or contract its central opening, the pupil. Moreover, eyelids are very generally added externally as additional screens. Yet the *origin* and *nature* of the parts of the vertebrate paired eye are very different from those of the similar parts in the cuttle-fish. The primary eye-chamber, or eyeball, of the vertebrate is a vesicle or hollow outgrowth of the wall of the hollow, tube-like primitive brain (see Fig. 34), and not a shallow, cup-like up-growth of the outer skin, as is that of the cuttle-fish (see Fig. 35). It is, strictly, a sac-like side-chamber of the brain. The lens of the vertebrate paired eye is *not* formed by the condensation of the viscid contents of the primary optic chamber, as in cuttle-fishes, but is a distinct cellular growth made up of many elongated cells which arises from the cell-layer of the outer skin or epidermis (Fig. 34,

A and B). It differs thus from all eyes which have a structureless lens formed by a surface deposit or secretion. Some of the bivalve molluscs (the Scallop or Pecten and others) have eyes provided with a multicellular lens like that of the paired eye of Vertebrates and of the pineal

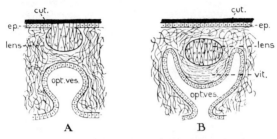

FIG. 34.—Diagrams of the actual development of one of the paired eyes of a Vertebrate.

A, earlier stage, showing the lens as a separate growth of the cells of the epidermis, and the optic vesicle (*opt.ves.*) as a hollow outgrowth of the wall of the brain cavity.

B, later stage, showing the lens now detached from the epidermis, and sinking into the cup formed by an in-pushing of the optic vesicle. Letters as follows : *cut.*, the cuticle ; *ep.*, the cellular epidermis ; *lens*, the cellular lens ; *opt.ves.*, the primitive optic vesicle, or outgrowth of the hollow brain. It becomes " invaginate " or cupped, and the cup becomes the " optic chamber " of Fig. 32, and is filled with a jelly-like growth (*vit.*), the vitreous humour. The double wall of the cup—so formed—becomes the retina (*ret.* of Fig. 32).

or third eye. Yet further, the primitive optic chamber of the vertebrate's paired eye differs greatly from that of most (if not all) other eyes in the fact that in the course of its growth in the embryo it very soon ceases to be a vesicle or chamber. The front half becomes pushed into the back half, so that the chamber becomes a double-walled sac of hemispherical shape (Fig. 34, B).

The formation of this new hemispherical chamber is accompanied by the separation of the lens from the skin, and by its taking up a position in the mouth of the hemispherical chamber. The double wall of the new chamber now loses *all trace of the original cavity* between its two layers, and the cells of which it consists become the elaborate " retina " of the eye, whilst the stalk of the chamber becomes the optic nerve. The hard coat of the eyeball, its dark lining or choroid, the anterior chamber, cornea, iris, and ciliary or focusing muscle, and the jelly (" vitreous humour ") of the posterior chamber now form around the lens by growth into the double-walled invaginated optic vesicle. It is obvious that there is *a similar modelling* of the parts of the vertebrate paired eye and of those of the cuttle-fish's paired eye, but not a deep-seated, genetic identity of

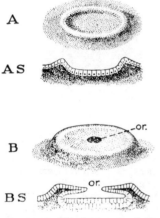

Fig. 35.—Development of the eye of a Cuttle-Fish. A, earliest ring-like up-growth. AS, section through the same. B, later stage; the ring closing in forming a chamber with central orifice (as in Nautilus) and finally closing up. BS, section of the same; *or*, orifice. (From the original description by E. R. L.)

the parts—lens, iris, cavities—compared. They are " homoplastic " (that is, of identical modelling) but not " homogenetic " (that is, not of identical origin or ancestry).

This brief consideration of other eyes—necessarily very rapid and sketchy—has been made in order that we

may arrive at some further appreciation of the " parietal "
or " pineal " or " third " eye of the lizard. Does it
conform in essentials to the pattern of the vertebrate
paired eyes ? Does it agree more closely with the
simple eyes of snails ? Or with that of the scorpion ?

The fact is that the lizard's parietal, or third, eye differs
in one or other important point from each of those we
have considered. It is small and dwindled, and probably
has lost some accessory parts which were present in the
big parietal eye of extinct reptiles. It agrees with the
fully formed snail's eye and the vertebrate paired eye
in being a closed chamber—an eyeball—with an optic
nerve attached to it. Like the vertebrate's paired eye, it
is a sac-like outgrowth of the hollow brain, but it does
not become tucked into itself or " invaginate." It remains
as the single chamber of the eye. The lens is formed by
elongate interlaced cells, as is that of the vertebrate
paired eye. It is a cell-structured lens, not a structureless
secretion like that formed in the chamber of the snail's
eye and of the cuttle-fish's eye, nor like the surface knob
of horny substance of the scorpion's eye. Nevertheless,
the lens of the lizard's parietal eye differs also greatly
from that of the vertebrate's paired eye. For, as shown
in our drawing of a section through it (Fig. 27), it is
merely a transparent thickening of the cellular growth
which forms the front wall of the simple eye-chamber or
eyeball itself. It is not a separately formed cellular
growth of the epidermis which moves into position from
the outside, as is the lens of the vertebrate paired eye
(Fig. 34). That makes a great difference between them.
In fact, the cell-structure of the lens is the only important
point in which they really agree, whilst differing from the
eyes of the snail, the cuttle-fish, and the scorpion. So
we have to regard the little parietal eye as quite apart in

the more profound and significant origin of its structural elements. Curiously enough, little eyes occur on the fringe of the soft " mantle " of the scallops and allied bivalve mussel-like molluscs, which are modified tentacles, and, whilst fairly simple in structure, have a lens which, like that of both the parietal and paired eyes of vertebrates, is not a structureless secretion, but shows " cell-structure "—that is to say, consists of a compacted growth of living cell units, as does the lens of the vertebrate's eyes.   The eyes in the back of some marine slugs, the rows of beautiful minute eyes discovered by Moseley in the series of shells situated on the back of the curious little chitons of the seashore, the eyes of starfishes, of sea-urchins, and of jelly-fish, each call for special description in a survey of the various kinds of eye-structure presented by animals.   We may return to them on some future occasion.   Enough has been here said of other eyes to enable the reader to appreciate the character and importance of the vertebrate's third eye.

CHAPTER XIV

WASPS

MOST people dislike wasps because, owing to blundering on their own part or that of a wasp, they have at some time or other experienced the acute pain caused by the wasp's sting. But those who have an eye for beauty recognize the grace, agility, and concentrated power of the brilliant little creature with its black-and-yellow livery and surprisingly tight-drawn waist. We must also score in its favour that it is cleanly and has no nasty smell as have some stingless insects, protecting them from aggression in the same way as its terrible stink-gland protects the skunk ; also that it will let you alone if you do not needlessly worry it. The worst that can be said of the wasp is that it nibbles and so injures ripe fruit which we wish to keep for ourselves, and that if you let one crawl up under your sleeve or trouser, or between your neck and collar, it resents your carelessness in permitting it to wander into such confined quarters, and irritably and recklessly stabs your soft warm flesh with its poisoned tail-sting.

Men and boys as a rule owe their painful experience of wasp's stings to their own clumsy attempts to destroy a wasps' nest, and the consequent legitimate defence and retaliation of the outraged wasps. We used, when I was a boy, to stuff a quantity of gunpowder or a couple of " squibs " into the mouth of the subterranean chamber in which the wasps had built their nest, and then set fire to a fuse. After the explosion, and when most of the wasps within the subterranean cave were either dead or stupefied, we used recklessly to dig out the " comb " and destroy with our spades the grubs and rare survivors. Usually these destructive attacks were made after sunset, when all the wasps had retired for the night ; and some of us were sure to be stung in the legs by half-stupefied victims crawling over the grass and seeking refuge between their assailant's leg and trouser. On one occasion we thus destroyed a nest during broad daylight in a river's bank, and were attacked by hundreds of the furious inhabitants who had not been within the nest, but returned to it when we were at work. They " charged " us like cavalry, and pursued us for a quarter of a mile, giving us much effective punishment with their stings ; and no doubt we deserved it, though we thought we were doing public service ! A better method than that of gunpowder has become usual of late years. Now-a-days when night has fallen and the nest is full, you place an ounce or so of cyanide of potassium well into the mouth of the little cave in which the wasps have built their nest, squirt on to it with a garden syringe a pint or so of water, close the hole tightly with a turf or ball of clay, and leave it. The poisonous fumes of the wet cyanide pervade the nest and kill all—young and old— within. Leave it alone afterwards ! A forgetful wasp destroyer omitted to inject the necessary water, and when next day in the presence of friends he triumphantly removed the closing turf from the mouth of the sepulchre, expecting to find all dead and silent within, he was attacked by the entire community who issued in swarms uninjured from the nest.

Those who are " worried " by wasps should avoid

them and try to draw them away from sitting-rooms by placing some attractive sweet stuff outside at a distance whilst covering all such edibles in the house or on the tea-table by a light cloth. It is useless to kill a few intruders, since as many as 30,000 are hatched out in a wasp's nest in the season. A really effective thing is to kill the few " queens," which make their appearance early in the spring. Each of these is the possible progenitor of several thousand in the warmer months.

Wasps eat not only sugar and fruits, but are carnivorous. They catch and carry off as food many injurious flies, caterpillars, and other insects ; they frequent butchers' shops not only to eat the meat, but also the blowflies which visit those establishments. They are thus largely " beneficial." Besides the damage which they do to fruit, some of them destroy young shoots and woody parts of trees in order, by munching the fibre, to make the paper-like paste of which their nests and brood-cells are constructed. This is especially the habit of that large kind of wasp—happily not very common— known as the hornet. The hornet has more than six times the bulk of the common wasp, and is alarming at close quarters on account of its loud buzz and rapid flight. I do not know of any account of the sting of a hornet showing it to be more serious than that of the common wasp, but a naturalist cannot be blamed for unwillingness to settle this point by experiment

Besides the common wasp and the hornet there are five other kinds or species of wasp met with in Britain, and some hundreds of foreign kinds. The British kinds include the German wasp (a digging wasp or trench maker), the red wasp, and the tree wasps, which build their turnip-shaped paper nests exposed to view on the branches of trees.   The hornet builds its papier-maché nest in hollow trees and outhouses.

The most interesting facts which the naturalist has to tell about wasps relate to their yellow and black colouring, to their stings, and to their social habits or " communities."   The yellow and black colour bands of a wasp's body are what are called " warning colours." They are avoided by birds, lizards, and other animals, since these colours accompany the poisonous sting.   The brilliant yellow-and-black " salamander " (a sort of newt common on the Continent, but not native here) secretes a deadly crystalline poison in its skin (as also does the common toad), and no animal which has taken one into its mouth and suffered accordingly will tackle the yellow-and-black gentry again.   The salamander slowly and confidently walks abroad in his yellow-and-black livery, safe from attack.   Some caterpillars, *e.g.* that of the cinnabar moth, as well as the common wasp, sport the poison colours—yellow and black—in alternate bands, and are consequently " let alone " by small carnivorous animals, who have learnt to fear them. Similarly the silver-grey back of the poison-squirting skunk is known to all his neighbours, even to horses and men, and they get out of his way.   He slowly paces along a road without fear, and ready to explode with acrid offence.   Insects of quite distinct orders, such as the two-winged hover-flies and the hornet-fly, and one of the clear-wing moths, though themselves innocuous, are protected from the attacks of other insects and larger animals by the close resemblance to the wasp given to them by the black and yellow bands of colour on their bodies.   They are exhibited in a special case in the Natural History Museum.

The sting of the wasp, like that of the bee and the ant, and other allied insects, has been derived in the long course of ages from a sharp piercing instrument present in the females of the more primitive members of this class of insects (the Hymenoptera) for use as a " borer " to make holes in the shoots of plants (the saw-flies and gall-flies), or in the bodies of caterpillars (the ichneumon flies), wherein to lay their eggs. The young are hatched from the eggs thus introduced into a plant-shoot or an animal, and feed upon it. What was an apparatus for providing for the safety and nutrition of the young, has in the stinging kinds lost that application, and by the addition to it of a poison gland, has become a powerful weapon of offence and defence. But it is still the peculiar possession of the females. The poison gland of the wasps, bees, and ants secretes both a narcotic or paralysing poison and formic acid. It is the formic acid which causes the pain we experience when stung. The poison alone, though it can paralyse a small insect, has in the quantities present neither painful nor toxic action upon man. It is a curious fact that the stinging hairs of the common nettle also emit both formic acid and a nerve-poison. Ammonia in not too strong solution is the best antidote to the acid sting of wasp or bee. A really dangerous result may be caused by the swelling of the tongue when stung by a wasp blundering into the open mouth of man, or woman, or child. A wineglassful of glycerine held in the mouth gives immediate relief Some kinds of ants have lost the sharp piercing sting whilst retaining the poison gland, and there are in South America certain kinds of " stingless " bees, in which the parts of the sting are reduced and useless for piercing.

Wasps and bees are closely related. Our common

wasp and the honey-bee, and many other kinds of both wasps and bees, form communities of which a " queen," or fertile female, is the foundress, and is assisted in the construction of the comb or aggregation of " cells " in which she lays her eggs by infertile or aborted females— the " workers." In the common wasp, as in the honey-bee, the workers relieve the queen of all labour, not only building the comb, but collecting and storing food for the nourishment of the young which are hatched as grubs from the eggs laid by the queen in separate cells. They emerge from their cells as " workers " or " queens " according to the food supplied to them by the adult workers of the community, or as " drones " (males) if the egg is not fertilized by the sperm received into her sperm-sac by the queen from a drone in a preceding season. Unlike that of the hive bees, the wasp's community is annual, existing for one summer only. All of its members die in the autumn, excepting a few queens (fully-formed females), which have been fertilized in the early autumn by the drones whilst flying high in the air. These creep into crevices under stones or trees and hibernate until the warmth of spring revives them. Each then sets to work independently to find some burrow or hole in the ground in which to build a nest. It is made of wood-pulp chewed by her, and consists at first of three—only three—shallow cup-like cells. In each of these an egg is laid. They hatch out as grubs and are fed by their mother on munched insects and honey, and develop into " workers," who build more cells, and provide more food for the new grubs, as does the queen also. She is now, however, mainly occupied in laying an egg in each cell as soon as it is completed. Thus the family community grows, and as the summer comes on the cells are counted in hundreds and thousands. Each may be used three times in the season, the queen providing an egg for each empty cell. The egg in less than three weeks becomes a full-grown wasp—a hard-working member of the fraternity—numbering from 10,000 to 20,000—all children of one parent ! The "communities" of bees and ants have a history and nature similar to that just sketched—varying in several important details. It seems at first sight unlikely that this system of family communities, consisting of queen, workers, and drones, each playing their own peculiar part with wonderful precision and exactness, can have arisen more than once in the course of development and the origin of new "species" by the selection of favoured races in the struggle for existence. It would at first sight seem probable that wasps, bees, and ants had inherited this highly organized system from one common original stock, which was, to begin with, of solitary habits (that is to say, united in isolated pairs to build each its own nest and rear its own young—as most insects and other animals do), and gradually acquired the communal habit and the limitation of egg-laying and other special activities as the task of special kinds or "castes" of the populous family. But the fact that there are well-known "solitary" species of wasps and of bees, and even of ants, and also in each of these groups —species or kinds which have only arrived at intermediate steps (leading towards the development of the large and completely organized communities seen in the common wasp, the honey-bee, and many species of ants), favours the conclusion that the groups known as wasps, bees, and ants have each independently given rise to community-forming or "social" species. This view is confirmed by the fact that insects of a widely separate order—the termites, of tropical and sub-tropical regions (confusingly called white "ants," for they are not ants)—also have developed an elaborate social system of the same kind, their communities consisting of millions of individuals of

9

males, queens, and workers, and often forming nests as big as a motor-bus.

The insects we have named wasps, bees, ants, and termites are the only insects which form such communities. Not only that, they are the only animals of any kind which form such communities. The resemblances to and wide differences from human societies presented by these insect communities form a subject of great philosophical and political significance.

CHAPTER XV

AN UNWARRANTED FANCY

SOME years ago I wrote in the " Daily Telegraph ' in reference to the notion entertained by some people that human beings can communicate with one another by a mysterious process which they cal " telepathy " as follows : " The hypothesis that any animal, including man, is affected ' sensorially ' through any channel excepting the known sense-organs is one of the truth of which no proof has ever been given in any case. No such proof has been given in the supposed instances of communication between human beings at a distance from one another." This statement attracted the attention of Mr. William Archer, who did not agree with me, and wrote a remarkable article in the " Daily News " on the subject. Mr. Archer is a versatile writer, and it is interesting to know how the pretensions to and beliefs in " thought-transference " are judged by one who has the exceptional opportunities which he has, for addressing the public on a matter of serious concern. Moreover, there is need for considering the matter again to-day—since those who believe in " telepathy " are still numerous, although no attempts to demonstrate its existence by decisive evidence have been successful. The existence of the belief in " telepathy " is in fact explained—as is the belief in ghosts, spirit-rapping, and other such fancies—by common and well-known causes.

The chief is ignorance of the necessity for carefully testing human testimony or evidence before accepting it. This, accompanied by coincidence, faulty observation and memory, victimization by fraud, mental disease resulting in illusion and hallucination, accounts for the persistence of these irrational and injurious fancies.

It is, of course, understood that Mr. Archer (as is obvious from his article) has no special knowledge of past and present beliefs in thought-reading, clairvoyance, and second sight referred to as supposed " communications of mind with mind otherwise than by means of the organs of sense." Nor does he come to the matter in hand as an expert in psychology, nor as a physiologist, nor as having the experience of a medical man. It is therefore not possible to discuss his statements and opinions on this matter as having any special weight. At the same time, they seem to me quite interesting, as showing the recklessness with which some people jump to conclusions on obscure and difficult matters requiring investigation, the inaccuracy with which they quote the statements of those who oppose their prejudices, and the effrontery with which they " bluff " by boldly asserting that those who do not agree with them are " behind the times." The assertion made by Mr. Archer that the opponents of credulity are " behind the times " is true only in so far as it is the fact that the times are exceptional on account of the present willingness of an uneducated public to accept as true the absurdities dished up for it by a certain class of writers, and in the loss of a sense of public duty and dignity, which until recently restrained the employers of such writers from seeking commercial success by disseminating injurious rubbish in magazines and newspapers.

We may take Mr. Archer as a sample of the credulous person who, in virtue of his want of method and experience, is imposed upon by pretensions to " occult " powers.   Such persons are still numerous, though less so than formerly.   Mr. Archer's credulity is less injurious to the public interest than the hardihood with which— though in no way qualified to do so—he declares, without offering a tittle of evidence in support of his statement, that the opinion of those qualified to judge on these matters has greatly changed since 1870 (why 1870 ?) and that " the man who, in these days, can doubt the transference of ideas from mind to mind, without any intervention of the recognized sense-organs, shows a heroic resolve to admit no evidence of a later date than 1870."   This is a complete misconception.

As a matter of fact, the further we go back in history the more general do we find the belief in such fancies as thought-transference and the accompanying superstitions as to apparitions, ghosts, and so-called " spiritualism," and the less do we find to be the knowledge of the facts as to the working of the human mind and as to the various physical phenomena by misunderstanding of which mankind has been led into erroneous and injurious beliefs.   The increase of knowledge and the destruction of the ignorance and misconception which has bolstered up superstition and the fanciful notions passed on to us from our primitive ancestors, have not ceased, as Mr. Archer unwarrantably asserts, but have largely progressed during the last fifty years.   We know much more of the working of the human and animal " mind " (the science called " psychology," not to be confused with sham science put forward under the same name) than we did in 1870, and more of the history and explanation of human fanciful beliefs and superstitions.   The repeated attempts of the credulous folk and their leaders—often corrupt impostors—to spread their beliefs have been met (by myself and others), and their false pretensions exposed, again and again—whenever, in fact, the credulous ones have submitted any of the marvels in which they believe to the test of decisive scientific experiment. The fact is that when Mr. Archer talks of the " evidence " since 1870 being in favour of " occultism," he chooses to call mere " testimony " or " assertion " by that name, whether it is false evidence or true evidence. He does not mean " evidence " which has been strictly tested by approved methods and declared by capable impartial judges to be entitled to belief.

Let us now take the example of what Mr. Archer considers to be evidence which (to use his own words) " proves " (that is Mr. Archer's word) " that there are means of communication between mind and mind, un-recognized and unaccounted for by orthodox science." He tells us of an exhibition of supposed powers of thought-transference given by a man and his daughter, at which he was present. The father, having left the room, the daughter, in a whisper, mentions to those persons in the room some real or imaginary scene she has called to mind, which he, returning, deciphers usually with scarcely a moment's pause. I give only one example of three narrated by Mr. Archer. The father having left the room, the daughter says she is thinking of " Miss Wilkins at the Winchester and Eton match, and grand-father dropping the cigar-end on her umbrella." The father, on returning to the room, says : " I feel as if this was still about Henry Wilkins, whom I have been talking about—and I have a feeling of grandfather. It is grotesque—grandfather dropping hot cigar-ash on an umbrella in the open air. Oh yes ! at the match at

Winchester." The other two cases are similar. It is on such " evidence " as this that Mr. William Archer asks people to believe that a thing, in any case, so unusual and so improbable as the transference of thoughts from mind to mind without the intermediary of one of the organs of sense actually takes place. It seems a mere waste of time after this to say anything more about the notions and assertions of Mr. Archer. Apparently, no precaution was taken by him to prevent lip-reading, none to prevent previous agreement between father and daughter as to the subjects to be guessed, and yet Mr. Archer says he believes, and asks us to believe, that the trick is done by thought-transference, without the use of sense-organs, and is a " proof " of its existence.

Let us for a moment realize the position. The only fact before us is that this relation is made in a daily paper over the signature " William Archer." What are the possible explanations of that fact ? I will take them in haphazard order. They are : (1) that the whole thing is imaginary, invented by a writer whose name is not William Archer ; (2) that William Archer did write the story and invented it to amuse his readers ; (3) that he believes it to be true in all its details, but was grossly deceived by the father and daughter ; (4) that Mr. Archer is mad, and honestly believes his story, which, however, is either wholly imaginary or is so in important details ; (5) that either the father or the daughter is insane, and is consequently allowed to carry on a deception which Mr. Archer failed to detect ; (6) that the story is quite true, and that thoughts can be transferred from brain to brain without the intermediary of any of the organs of sense.

Of these possible explanations of the fact before us, namely, the story printed in the " Daily News " over Mr.

Archer's name, it must, most distinctly, be stated that the most improbable is the last. No one claiming to be considered a reasonable being can possibly accept conclusion No. 6 until it has been demonstrated that each of the other five suggested explanations must be excluded. Any one of them is more probable—that is to say, is more in accordance with recorded human experience—than the last. It would be quite easy to test these hypothetical explanations, and until this is carried out by trustworthy and careful observers I recommend my readers to dismiss the whole childish history from their minds.

It is, of course, useless for one who has such loose ideas as to the value of " evidence " and the nature of " proof " as Mr. Archer betrays in the narrative of what he calls his " researches in telepathy," to talk about the evidence existing before 1870, and that which has accumulated since that date. Like many other people, Mr. Archer has never learnt how to test " evidence " and what constitutes " proof " and " demonstration." I must also point out that Mr. Archer makes (as many people do) a confusion between what is possible and what is proved. He seems to think that what he conceives as possible is already made probable or is even " proved." And on the other hand, by a similar process of confusion, he makes a baseless charge against me. He writes : " Sir Ray Lankester simply denies that any communication can occur between mind and mind, except through one or other of the five known avenues of sense." This is a piece of carelessness on Mr. Archer's part. I do nothing of the kind. I make a point of avoiding dogmatic statements as to what " can " or " cannot " be. I am concerned with " that which is." The statement of mine which Mr. Archer has perverted is that quoted at the beginning of this chapter, in which I do not say that no such communication "can" occur between mind and mind, but that "no proof" of its occurrence has ever been given in any case. That is a totally different thing. It is no prophecy, but a simple statement of fact, which can be met by exhibiting the proof demanded—the experimental proof—at any moment before a competent jury of scientific experts. Mr. Archer apparently does not appreciate the difference between my statement and his version of it. He is content to offer—to a confiding public—a worthless experiment—worthless because carelessly and ignorantly made—as a "proof" of the existence of communication between mind and mind, by a channel other than that afforded by the known organs of sense. And in an equally reckless spirit he misrepresents the words of one who rejects his unwarranted suppositions.

It is necessary to remind those who continue to assert that "telepathy" is a frequent occurrence and ask us to prove that it is not—or else to admit that it is—that their method is universally condemned. It is for them to bring *conclusive evidence* demonstrating the truth of their contention. This they have not done, but instead challenge their opponents to prove that they are wrong. This is an old trick which still deceives the unwary—but has long ago been recognized as the resort of those who are unable to establish an assertion by trustworthy evidence.

CHAPTER XVI

SPIDER-SENSE AND CAT-SENSE

THERE is at the present day a more general disposition than was the case thirty or forty years
ago to dabble in " occultism "—to seriously
relate and discuss stories and theories as to ghosts,
divination, second sight, and mysterious inherited
memories of long-past ages. This change of attitude
is not accounted for by any discoveries of a scientific
nature tending to give support to popular superstitions
or to so-called " occultism." The fact is that there is a
distinct lowering in the standard of veracity and sound
common sense which not long ago characterized the best
English journalism. Newspapers, formerly written for
serious men, now not unfrequently cater for those who
desire tit-bits of scandal, and also for lovers of pseudo-
scientific mysteries and medical quackery decked out
with sham learning and airs of profundity.

Among the mysteries thus offered to the contemplation of the public is one which has been dubbed the
" spider-sense." It is related that there are persons
who not only have an extreme and unaccountable dread
and dislike of spiders, but that some of them are brought
into a strange state of nervous agitation by the proximity
of a spider, and may even faint in consequence. Not
only is this extreme nervous disturbance reported, but it

is further stated that such individuals are thus affected by the presence of a spider in the same room with them, even when it is not seen by the sufferer nor its presence suspected by others. The susceptible individuals have insisted on a search being made for the unseen spider, and it is stated by witnesses present on such occasions that after hunting about in corners and among shelves the offending spider has been discovered and ejected, whereupon the agitated individual (a la ly in one case) has recovered serenity. On this basis we are seriously, and with an air of exceptional learning, asked to admit the existence of a peculiar sense—not that of sight, of hearing, of smell, of taste, or of the various kinds grouped as " touch " (enumerated in Chapter X). This peculiar " sense " is assumed to be possessed by some individuals and not by others, and to enable those individuals to recognize the presence of a spider when other persons cannot do so. It is proposed to call this the " spider-sense," and by the more elaborately phantastic of these wonder-mongers the manifestation is compared to recorded cases in which a cat takes the place of the spider, and we are gravely assured that there is a " cat-sense " which is similar to but, of course, not identical with, the " spider-sense." Both " spider-sense " and " cat-sense " are, it seems probable, a variety of non-sense !

We have in the narratives just referred to, a statement of what is undoubtedly correct observation of fact, to which is added an altogether gratuitous and fanciful assumption, which it is declared is a necessary, or at any rate a very probable, " explanation " of the facts. The facts, which are perfectly well known, are that individuals —men as well as women—are not uncommonly met with who have curiously intense fear of, or dislike for, certain animals or certain things, the dislike causing so great a disturbance of the nervous system that the affected individual will violently seek to escape from the presence of the horror-causing animal or thing, and may scream and exhibit other signs of distress, or may faint. The mere sight of blood has this effect on some people ; they faint—that is to say, the nervous disturbance is such as to cause an arrest of the contractions of the heart and the supply of blood to the brain. Even the word " blood " has that effect upon some people, whilst medical men find that many persons when lightly scratched on the arm in " vaccination," faint if the merest trace of blood appears. The sight or touch of a snake, even of a harmless kind, produces excessive and uncontrollable terror in some men and women, and also in some monkeys. A curious effect of a " shocking " sight is one to which I was myself subject in youth. If I saw anyone with red, inflamed eyes and everted eyelids (beggars used to exhibit themselves in that condition in the streets of London), my own eyes at once became painful and suffused with liquid. Some people are thrown into an unreasoning state of terror (as most of us have had occasion to observe) when led into a subterranean passage or dungeon, and not infrequently faint in consequence. Others exhibit a morbid horror of wide, open spaces, whilst proximity to the edge of a precipice produces in some persons excessive terror and physical collapse. A number of such individual peculiarities could be mentioned. They have been studied, and their nature and origin more or less satisfactorily explained by medical men. They are individual and unhealthily exaggerated reactions of mental impressions upon the activity of various organs of the body by means of the nerves which supply those organs.

The special and exaggerated discomfort or even

terror which some common animals produce in certain persons belongs to this class of individual peculiarities of the nervous apparatus.   Women very usually in this part of the world are thrown into a state of nervous terror by the presence in a room of an uncaged mouse. Apparently this is due not to any instinctive dislike on the part of women to a mouse, but to a fear cultivated by stories told by them to one another from early childhood of the possibility of a mouse, when alarmed and running about here and there in order to escape danger, with a rapidity rendering it invisible, suddenly seeking shelter in their skirts.   The imagination has been cultivated in regard to this possibility to such a degree that a mouse has become a bogy.   Less commonly a bat is an object of special terror on account of its occasionally getting itself entangled in a woman's hair.   I am inclined to think that the rapidly and suddenly moving spider has in the same way established itself as a bogy—especially where country-folk have added to its terrors by unfounded assertions that its bite is poisonous to man. As a matter of fact, though spiders have poison-producing fangs, with which they can stab and paralyse their minute prey, there is no evidence of any European spider causing injury to a human being in this way.   Many naturalists have made experiments with different species of spiders and have failed to experience any but the most trifling inconvenience from their bites—less than that caused by a bee-sting or the stab of a mosquito.

The whole story of the " Tarantula "—a fairly large spider common in Italy and known to naturalists as Lycosa tarentula—which receives its name from the town of Taranto, is now discredited.   It was believed that the bite of this spider caused a peculiar sleepiness and also painful symptoms in men and women, only to be

cured by music, which set the bitten victim dancing.
The dance was called the " Tarantella." Goldsmith,
the delightful writer of stories and plays, declared in
his " Animated Nature " that the whole thing was an
elaborate imposture on the part of the Tarantese peasants
who, for a fee paid by a credulous traveller, would be
bitten, simulate apparent collapse, and then pretend to
be restored by music and the violent dancing of the
" tarantella," which, they declared, they felt mysteriously
compelled to perform.   It was supposed that the sweating
caused by the exertion freed the body of the poison.
Probably some tradition, from early Roman times, as to
the dire effects of spiders' bites, may have had to do with
the imposture, but it is also probable that the curious
" dancing-mania " (described in Shakespeare's play of
" King Lear "), which spread through Europe in the
Middle Ages, and is spoken of as " Tarantism," was
connected with the introduction of an imaginary danger
from the spider's bite and its equally imaginary cure by
dancing.

The chief modern authority on spiders was the late
Rev. Henry M'Cook, D.D., of Philadelphia. I am indebted to his kindness for a copy of his great book on
American spiders, published in 1889. He inquired into
the subject of poisonous bites by various species of
spiders very carefully, and experimented on himself.
He thinks it probable that the large " bird's-nesting "
spiders of the tropics (often and misleadingly called by
the old name " Tarantula ") are capable of inflicting a
poisonous wound on man, causing as much injury as the
sting of a scorpion. He considers that the size of the
animal and the statements made to him render this
probable, but has never seen a case himself, though he
has handled many living specimens of these large spiders.

The most definite statements which he cites concerning spiders' bites are those as to " black spiders," species of the genus Latrodectus (little bigger than a large specimen of our common garden spider), which are found in New Zealand, in the Southern States of North America, and in North Africa. A carefully recorded case of serious illness apparently due to a bite of this kind of spider was given to Dr. M'Cook by a New Zealand settler, and two cases are recorded of negroes bitten in South Carolina, one of which terminated fatally. But, on the other hand, a well-known naturalist, M. Lucas, experimenting in Algeria, allowed this kind of spider to bite him on many occasions, and suffered no inconvenience. None of the reports of serious results were quite satisfactory, for the spider was not clearly shown to have been the actual offender, although found near the injured person. The bite may really have been that of a snake, the proximity of which was unobserved and unsuspected.

Dr. M'Cook states that even in attacking their prey spiders do not always make use of their poison, and that insects when swathed and bound by spiders in their threads frequently are not paralysed or poisoned at all, but remain capable of movement and recovery when liberated. He concludes that the poison is only exceptionally used as a reserve weapon by spiders, and that its virulence probably depends on the physiological condition of the spider and its degree of excitement, while its effect is very largely determined by the actual state of health of the individual bitten. On the whole, we must conclude that the belief that any spiders do actually inflict poisonous bites on human beings is an example of that strange terror-stricken imagination which is prevalent in barbarous peoples, and in earlier times was common in Europe, and has largely survived to this day. For instance, the country-folk in Suffolk believe that if you take hold of a toad your hand will wither and become paralysed. It is true that the skin of the toad secretes a poison which has an acrid taste and is so virulent that a dog drops a toad with every evidence of pain and terror should he take one into his mouth. But the skin of the human hand is not affected by this poison, and there is no ground for the belief that it can be paralysed or withered by contact with a toad. These curious examples of credulity among learned and unlearned alike belong rather to the natural history of man than to that of the animals concerning which such stories are told.

We thus are led to bring the exaggerated dread of spiders into line with other ill-grounded antipathies and horrors caused by harmless bogies. But we have yet to examine the statement that persons who have this antipathy to spiders are able to detect—in consequence of the peculiar nervous agitation set up in them—the presence of a spider in a room when no spider has been seen in that room, and when other persons present have no suspicion of its presence. The evidence on this point is altogether insufficient to establish the existence of such a power. In a room in the middle of London no amount of searching would reveal the presence of a spider unless it had been purposely brought there. In any house in the country careful search would, more probably than not, lead to the discovery of one or more spiders in any room. Therefore, if a fanciful nervous person finds himself (or herself) occupying a room in some country house where spiders are likely to be concealed, it is not surprising that the suitability of the place should suggest their presence, and the consequent nervous agitation ensue. It is also not surprising that one or more spiders should be discovered in the room when a search is made. There is no need to assume the existence in the agitated individual of any peculiar capacity for the detection of spiders, even such as a specially acute sense of smell or hearing, let alone a " sixth sense "—a " spider sense." Such an assumption is unreasonable and fantastic. Its truth could be easily put to the test by placing in different rooms of a London house several perforated boxes, in one of which the experimenter has concealed a spider. Anyone with a special sense or sensitiveness enabling him to recognize the presence of an unseen spider should be able to point out in which room and which box the spider is concealed. It is only by such an experiment, carefully carried out with precautions to avoid any ordinary indications as to where the spider has been concealed, that the existence of a " spider-sense " could be rendered probable, and if the result were favourable then the question would arise, " By which of the five gateways of sense has the spider made its presence felt ? " The hypothesis that any animal, including man, is affected " sensorially " through any channel excepting the known sense-organs is one of the truth of which no proof has ever been given in any case. The unwarranted belief that such communication by other channels than the organs of sense do take place is encouraged, on the part of lovers of mystification, in the minds of credulous persons by giving to these supposed occurrences a pretentious name which begs the question as to their reality —namely, " telepathy."

A parallel to the stories about sensitiveness to the unseen presence of spiders is afforded by those as to the dislike felt by many people to the common cat and the discomfort experienced by them in its presence—a discomfort which is believed by many to be excited by the presence of a cat unseen and unindicated by any of the recognized sense-organs. This curious aversion to the common cat does exist to an acute degree in many men and women. It is stated by those who feel it that it does not extend to the larger cats, such as the lion, tiger, and leopard. It probably arises from a fear and terror of the domestic cat—established in early childhood—by startling encounters with cats in dark rooms and the foolish talk by older people about the mysterious wickedness of these wandering nocturnal creatures. It is not surprising that anyone who is a victim of the " cat aversion " should now and then declare that he (or she) is sure that there is a cat in the room, although others present deny that there is, and then that, now and then, when search is made, poor puss is found curled up in some remote corner or on the top of a bookshelf ! The " ælurophobe " or " cat-hater " will often be mistaken, but sometimes right, and the cases when he was right will remain in his friends' memory, and those in which he was wrong will be forgotten. A good instance of successful " cat-discovery " was told to me by the distinguished Indian official, the late Sir Richard Strachey. He and his wife, many years ago, started on a long drive in India in a closed travelling carriage with a very great soldier, a well-known General. They had not proceeded more than twenty minutes when the General showed signs of discomfort, fidgeted, looked about the carriage, and at last said, " If I did not know it was impossible, I should say that there is a cat somewhere in this carriage." He maintained this attitude, and complained from time to time, until, after a couple of hours, the carriage drew up at the first halting-place. They all got out, and Sir Richard opened the luggage compartment at the back of the carriage, when out stepped a somewhat annoyed, but calm and dignified, domestic cat !

The inference immediately suggested by these un-doubted facts was that the General was gifted with a peculiar "cat-sense," and had thereby detected the presence of pussy in the rumble. Were we to accept this inference it would not be necessary to suppose that the "cat-sense" was anything more than a very acute and unusual sense of smell. We should, indeed, not be surprised at all by a dog thus detecting the presence of a cat or other animal concealed in a neighbouring compart-ment of a travelling carriage. And there is thoroughly good evidence that though mankind generally, and especially civilized man, has lost the acuteness of smell-perception which his early ancestors possessed, yet there are individuals in whom it is even now exceptionally keen, and further, that it may act so as to cause aversion or attraction without the individual so affected being conscious of the fact that he is being affected through his olfactory organs. Very interesting in this connection are the cases (of which I have seen instances) in which, during the hypnotic trance, the acuteness of the sense of smell is enormously increased, so that the hypnotized subject could name different odoriferous substances when brought, one by one, into a room in stoppered (but not hermetically sealed) bottles, though the olfactory sense of no one else was in the least degree affected.

But, on the whole, I do not think that we must con-clude that the General had a special acuteness of nose for the smell of a cat. He was known for his confessed aversion to cats, and his boast that he could detect the presence of one by the strange sensations of discomfort which it produced in him. The experiment had been tried on him before his drive with Sir Richard Strachey, and some of his young friends at the residence from which the carriage set forth were repeating an old performance when they put the cat in the rumble.   Is it more probable that the General unconsciously smelt the cat, or that he got an inkling of the experiment arranged by his young friends ?   In the latter case he must keep up his reputation, even should his suspicions, excited by their guilty faces and hurried movements about the back of the carriage, prove to be baseless.   So he accepted the notion that a cat had been placed in the carriage, became uncomfortable, and declared that were it not impossible he should say there was a cat in the carriage.   If no cat had been found, his friends and believers in his cat-finding powers would have said that there must have been one there the day before !   It is thus, it seems, clear that there is no ground for launching out into mystical theories of " spider-sense " and " cat-sense."   It is injurious to those who are liable to believe what they read, that such theories should be paraded by writers who do not even know or care what a sense or a sense-organ is, nor what is meant by the investigation of nature.

CHAPTER XVII

TWO EXPERIMENTS

RECENTLY a reference made by a public speaker to the attempt to put salt on a bird's tail reminded me of my first attempt, when I was seven years old, to deal experimentally with a popular superstition. I was a very trustful child, and I had been assured by various grown-up friends that if you place salt on a bird's tail the bird becomes as it were transfixed and dazed, and that you can then pick it up and carry it off. On several occasions I carried a packet of salt into the London park where my sister and I were daily taken by our nurse. In vain I threw the salt at the sparrows. They always flew away, and I came to the conclusion that I had not succeeded in getting any salt or, at any rate, not enough on to the tail of any one of them.

Then I devised a great experiment. There was a sort of creek 8 feet long and 3 feet broad at the west end of the ornamental water in St. James's Park. My sister attracted several ducks with offerings of bread into this creek, and I, standing near its entrance, with a huge paper bag of salt, trembled with excitement at the approaching success of my scheme. I poured quantities—whole ounces of salt—on to the tails of the doomed birds as they passed me on their way back from the creek to the open water. Their tails were covered with salt. But, to my surprise and horror, they did not stop! They gaily swam forward, shaking their feathers and uttering derisive "quacks." I was profoundly troubled and distressed. I had clearly proved one thing, namely, that my nursemaid, uncle, and several other trusted friends—but not, I am still glad to remember, my father—were either deliberate deceivers or themselves the victims of illusion. I was confirmed in my youthful wish to try whether things are as people say they are or not. Somewhat early perhaps, I adopted the motto of the Royal Society, *Nullius in verba*. And a very good motto it is, too, in spite of the worthy Todhunter and other toiling pedagogues, who have declared that it is outrageous to encourage a youth to seek demonstration rather than accept the statement of his teacher, especially if the latter be a clergyman. My experiment was on closely similar lines to that made by the Royal Society on July 24, 1660 —in regard to the alleged property of powdered rhinoceros horn—which was reputed to paralyse poisonous creatures such as snakes, scorpions, and spiders. We read in the journal-book, still preserved by the Society, under this date : " A circle was made with powder of unicorne's horn, and a spider set in the middle of it, but it immediately ran out severall times repeated. The spider once made some stay upon the powder."

A more interesting result followed from an experiment made in the same spirit twenty-five years later. I was in Paris, and went with a medical friend to visit the celebrated physician Charcot, to whom at that time I was a stranger, at the Salpêtrière Hospital. He and his assistants were making very interesting experiments on hypnotism. Charcot allowed great latitude to the young doctors who worked with him. They initiated and carried through very wild " exploratory " experiments on this difficult subject. Charcot did not discourage them, but did not accept their results unless established by unassailable evidence, although his views were absurdly misrepresented by the newspapers and wondermongers of the day.

At this time there had been a revival of the ancient and fanciful doctrine of "metallic sympathies," which flourished a hundred years ago, and was even then but a revival of the strange fancies as to "sympathetic powders," which were brought before the Royal Society by Sir Kenelm Digby at one of its first meetings, in 1660. In the journal-book of the Royal Society of June 5 of that year, we read, "Magnetical cures were then discoursed of. Sir Gilbert Talbot promised to bring in what he knew of sympatheticall cures. Those that had any powder of sympathy were desired to bring some of it at the next meeting. Sir Kenelm Digby related that the calcined powder of toades reverberated, applyed in bagges upon the stomach of a pestiferate body, cures it by several applications." The belief in sympathetic powders and metals was a last survival of the mediæval doctrine of "signatures," itself a form of the fetish believed in by African witch-doctors, and directly connected with the universal system of magic and witchcraft of European as well as of more remote populations. To this day, such beliefs lie close beneath the thin crust of modern knowledge and civilization, even in England, treasured in obscure tradition and ready to burst forth in grotesque revivals in all classes of society. The Royal Society put many of these reputed mechanisms of witchcraft and magic to the test, and by showing their failure to produce the effects attributed to them, helped greatly to cause witches, wizards, and their followers to draw in their horns and disappear. The germ, however, remained, and reappears in various forms to-day.

Thirty years ago some of the doctors in Paris believed that a small disc of gold, or copper, or of silver, laid flat on the arm, could produce an absence of sensation in the arm, and that whilst one person could be thus affected by one metal another person would respond only to another metal, according to a supposed " sympathy " or special affinity of the nervous system for this or that metal. This astonishing doctrine was thought to be proved by certain experiments made with the abnormally " nervous " women who frequent the Salpêtrière Hospital as out-patients. That the loss of sensation, which was real enough, was due to what is called " suggestion "—that is to say, a belief on the part of the patient that such would be the case, because the doctor said it would—and had nothing to do with one metal or another, was subsequently proved by making use of wooden discs in place of metallic ones, the patient being led to suppose that a disc of metal of the kind with which she believed herself " sympathetic " was being applied. Sensation disappeared just as readily as when a special metallic disc was used.

The old hypothesis of the influence of a magnet on the human body was at this time revived, and Charcot's pupils found that when a susceptible female patient held in the hand a bar of iron surrounded by a coil of copper wire leading to a chemical electric cell or battery nothing happened so long as the connection was broken. But as soon as the wire was connected so as to set up an electric current and to make the bar of iron into a magnet, the hand and arm (up to the shoulder) of the young woman holding the bar, lost all sensation. She was not allowed to see her hand and arm, and was apparently quite unconscious of the thrusting of large carpet-needles into, and even through, them, though as long as the bar of iron was not magnetized she shrunk from a pin-prick applied to the same part. I saw this experiment with Charcot and some others present, and I noticed that the order to an assistant to " make contact," that is to say, to convert the bar of iron into a magnet, was given very emphatically by Charcot, and that there was an attitude of expectation on the part of all present—which was followed by the demonstration by means of needle-pricking that the young woman's arm had lost sensation, or, as they say, " was in a state of anæsthesia."

Charcot went away saying he should repeat the experiment before some medical friends in an hour or two. In the meantime, being left alone in the laboratory with my companion as witness, I emptied the chemical fluid (potassium bichromate) from the electric battery and substituted pure water. It was now incapable of setting up an electric current and converting the bar into a magnet. When Charcot returned with his visitors, the patient was brought in, and the whole ritual repeated. There was no effect on sensation when the bar was held in the hand so long as the order to set the current going, and so magnetize the bar, had not been given. At last the word was given, " Make ! " An assistant quickly submerged the galvanic couple in the cell supposed to contain a solution of potassium bichromate, and at once the patient's arm became anæsthetized, as earlier in the day. We ran large carpet-needles into the hand without the smallest evidence of the patient's knowledge. The order was given to break the current (that is, to cease magnetizing the bar), and at once the young woman exhibited signs of discomfort, and remonstrated with Charcot for allowing such big needles to be thrust into her hand when she was devoid of sensation ! My experiment had succeeded perfectly.

It would not have done to let Charcot, or anyone else (except my witness), know that when the order " Make " was given, there was no " making," and that the bar remained as before un-magnetized because the active bichromate had been replaced by water. The conviction of every one, including Charcot himself, that the bar became a magnet, and that loss of sensation would follow, was a necessary condition of the " suggestion " or control of the patient. It was thus demonstrated that the state of the iron bar as magnet or not magnet had nothing to do with the result, but that the important thing was that the patient should believe that the bar became a magnet, and that she should be influenced by her expectation, and that of all those around her, that the bar, being now a magnet, sensation would disappear from her arm. With appropriate apologies I explained to Charcot that the electric battery had been emptied by me, and that no current had been produced. The assistants rushed to verify the fact, and I was expecting that I should be frigidly requested to take my leave, when my hand was grasped, and my shoulder held by the great physician, who said, " Mais que vous avez bien fait, cher Monsieur ! " I had many delightful hours with him in after years, both at the Salpêtrière and in his beautiful old house and garden in the Boulevard St. Germain.

There are few " subjects " in this country for the student of hypnotism to equal the patients of the Salpêtrière and other hospitals in France—and very few amongst those who read, and even write, about " occultism " and " super-normal phenomena " know the leading facts which have been established in regard to this important branch of psychology. The study of the natural history of the mind, its modes of activity, and its defects and diseases is of fundamental importance—

but its results are often either unknown or greatly misunderstood by those who have most need of such knowledge, namely, those who, mistaking the attitude of an ignorant child for that of " a candid inquirer," try to form a judgment as to the truth or untruth of stories of ghosts, thought-transference, spirit-controls, crystal-gazing, divining-rods, amulets, and the evil eye.

CHAPTER XVIII

THE LAST OF THE ALCHEMISTS

GREAT interest was excited fourteen years ago by the assertion in the daily press that a French experimenter had devised a secret process by means of which sugar could be converted in the laboratory into large marketable diamonds. The distinguished chemist, Moissan, had a few years earlier obtained very minute true diamonds by heating sugar to a very high temperature in a closed iron bomb placed in a furnace. This gave a certain plausibility to the pretended discovery. But, like the elusive " philosopher's stone " of the mediæval alchemists, which should convert base metals into gold, when fused with them, the modern diamond-maker's secret process proved to be a worthless fraud.

In England, after the true scientific spirit had been brought to bear on such inquiries by Robert Boyle and the founders of the Royal Society in the later years of the seventeenth century, little was heard of " alchemy," and the word " chemistry " took its place, signifying a new method of study in which the actual properties of bodies, their combinations and decompositions, were carefully ascertained and recorded without any prepossessions as to either the mythical philosopher's stone or the elixir of life. But as late as 1783—only a hundred and forty years ago—we come across a strange and tragic history in the records of the Royal Society associated with the name of James Price, who was a gentleman commoner of Magdalen Hall, Oxford. After graduating as M.A. in 1777, he was, at the age of twenty-nine, elected a Fellow of the Royal Society of London. In the following year the University of Oxford conferred on him the degree of M.D. in recognition of his discoveries in natural science, and especially for his chemical labours. Price was born in London in 1752, and his name was originally Higginbotham, but he changed it on receiving a fortune from a relative.

This fortunate young man, whose abilities and character impressed and interested the learned men of the day, provided himself with a laboratory at his country house at Stoke, near Guildford. Here he carried on his researches, and the year after that in which honours were conferred on him by his University and the great scientific Society in London, he invited a number of noblemen and gentlemen to his laboratory to witness the performance of seven experiments, similar to those of the alchemists—namely, the transmutation of baser metals into silver and into gold. The Lords Onslow, Palmerston, and King of that date were amongst the company. Price produced a white powder, which he declared to be capable of converting fifty times its own weight of mercury into silver, and a red powder, which, he said, was capable of converting sixty times its own weight of mercury into gold. The preparation of these powders was a secret, and it was the discovery of them for which Price claimed attention. The experiments were made. In seven successive trials the powders were mixed in a crucible with mercury, first **four crucibles, with weighed quantities of the white powder,** and then three other crucibles with weighed quantities of the red powder. Silver and gold appeared in the crucibles after heating in a furnace, as predicted by Price. The precious metal produced was examined by assayers and pronounced genuine. Specimens of the gold were exhibited to His Majesty King George III, and Price published a pamphlet entitled " An Account of Some Experiments, etc.," in which he repudiated the doctrine of the philosopher's stone, but claimed that he had, by laborious experiment, discovered how to prepare these composite powders, which were the practical realization of that long-sought marvel. He did not, however, reveal the secret of their preparation. The greatest excitement was caused by this publication appearing under the name of James Price, M.D. (Oxon.), F.R.S. It was translated into foreign languages, and caused a tremendous commotion in the scientific world.

Some of the older Fellows of the Royal Society, friends of Price, now urged him privately to make known his mode of preparing the powders, and pointed out the propriety of his bringing his discovery before the Society. But this Price refused to do. To one of his friends he wrote that he feared he might have been deceived by the dealers who had sold mercury to him, and that apparently it already contained gold. He was urged by two leading Fellows of the Society to repeat his experiments in their presence, and he thereupon wrote that the powders were exhausted, and that the expense of making more was too great for him to bear, whilst the labour involved had already affected his health, and he feared to submit it to a further strain. The Royal Society now interfered, and the president (Sir Joseph Banks) and officers insisted that " for the honour of the Society " he must repeat the experiments before delegates of the Society, and show that his statements were truthful and his experiments without fraud.

Under this pressure the unhappy Dr. Price consented to repeat the experiments. He undertook to prepare in six weeks ten powders similar to those which he had used in his public demonstration. He appears to have been in a desperate state of mind, knowing that he could not expect to deceive the experts of the society. He hastily studied the works of some of the German alchemists as a forlorn hope, trusting that he might chance upon a successful method in their writings. He also prepared a bottle of " laurel water, " a deadly poison. Three Fellows of the Royal Society came on the appointed day, in August 1783, to the laboratory, near Guildford. It is related (I hope it is not true) that one of them visited the laboratory the day before the trial, and, having obtained entrance by bribing the housekeeper in Price's absence, discovered that his crucibles had false bottoms and recesses in which gold or silver could be hidden before the quicksilver and powder were introduced. Dr. Price appears to have received his visitors, but whether he commenced the test experiments in their presence or not does not appear. When they were solemnly assembled in the laboratory he quietly drank a tumblerful of the laurel water (hydrocyanic acid), which he had prepared, and fell dead before them. He left a fortune of £12,000 in the Funds. It has been discussed whether Dr. Price was a madman or an impostor. Probably vanity led him on to the course of deception which ended in this tragic way. He could not bring himself to confess failure or deception, nor to abscond. He ended his trouble by suicide. He was only thirty-one years of age! Not inappropriately he has been called the " Last of the Alchemists," though a long interval of time separates him from the last but one and the days when the old traditions of the Arabians' " al-kimia " were really treasured and the mystic art still practised.

CHAPTER XIX

EXTREME OLD AGE

FROM time to time the self-control of some contemporary journalists suddenly gives way, and the natural tendency to write nonsense about supposed marvels proves too much for them. We have not, it is true, for some years been favoured with reports of the arrival of the great sea-serpent, nor have extinct monsters of enormous size been frequently discovered walking about in remote parts of the African continent. But three well-seasoned, oft-exploded, and ever-fascinating marvels may be expected at any moment to be re-born from their ashes in the newspaper Press. These are, first, the so-called " well-attested " cases of survival on the part of certain old men to the age of 130, 185, and even 207 years; secondly, the discovery of a " toad in a hole," which hops out of a block of coal, having been concealed therein, according to the wonder-mongers, for countless ages; thirdly, the pretended discoveries of subterranean water by the aid of " the divining rod "—that great instrument of the magic art— of the ancient use of and belief in which the modern trifler in " occultism " is apparently ignorant.[1]

---

[1] For some account of the belief as to the survival of pre-Adamite toads in slabs of rock or of coal, and for a brief discussion of the pretensions of " dowsers " and water-finders, see chapters xxxvi–xl of my book, " Diversions of a Naturalist " (Methuen, 1915).

Each of these marvels has, like " telepathy " or " second sight," and the extruding of " ectoplasmic " ghosts by enterprising mediums, been recently announced as a " discovery "—not, of course, for the first time. According to some wonder-mongers, whenever you tell a story asserting the existence of something new and astonishing, you " discover " it. That, however, is not —I need hardly say—the sense in which the word is used by scientific investigators. When Professor and Madame Curie " discovered " the wonderful element " radium " they placed it, so to speak, " on the table," and every one has been able to examine it and to prove that the statements made about it are true. When Dr. Laveran, of Paris, " discovered " that malarial fever is due to a parasite in the blood he showed the parasite, and showed how one can always find it, and thus he enabled anyone and every one to see it and to examine its relation to malarial fever. Those are instances of " discovery." Mere guesses and assertions without proof are not " discovery."

The whole subject of the possible and probable duration of an individual's life is one which has naturally great interest for mankind. Apart from the question of the duration of human life, we know that the kinds or species of animals and plants show great differences as compared with one another in regard to duration of life. Life is, as is universally recognized, a tender thing, and liable to be suddenly arrested and brought to a close by accident or disease at all ages. A vast proportion of living things perish in the first days of their existence, soon after they have been separated as germs, embryos, or incompletely grown " young " from the mother, of which they are detached bits or buds. If we speak of " the average duration of life " in any species we must include all the individuals born or separated from the parent, and since it is the fact that in the case of some animals and plants (for instance, in the case of the oyster and many worms) several million young are produced by each mother, of which on the average only one pair survive to maturity (if we take account of what goes on in all regions, favourable and unfavourable, where the species occurs), it is clear that the " average duration of life " must be very low in these species and very high where only a dozen young are produced by each mother In man in this country it has been shown to be, now, about fifty years. Consequently " the average duration of life " in any species, even if we know what length of time it is, does not tell us to what age an animal or plant, if it has escaped the dangers of childhood and arrived at maturity, may be expected to live, nor what age it may, in exceptional cases, possibly attain.

In the case of man we have in civilized States arrived at a means of forming a fairly accurate conclusion on these two points, in consequence of the keeping, by public authority, of registers of the actual population, of the number of individuals born annually, and of the number of deaths every year and of the ages at which these deaths have occurred. These important registers have not yet been kept, in an accurate way, for as much as a century, but they have been kept for a sufficient time to give broadly stated conclusions. The " expectation of life " (as it is called) at different ages can now be calculated in the more civilized communities, and great care has been given to collecting the statistics and reasoning from them correctly, because it is necessary for enabling life insurance associations to carry on their business, and also to enable the Government to form correct conclusions as to the value of public regulations in regard to sanitary legisla-

tion and the causes which affect the increase of population. Thus we have tables published more than fifty
years ago [1] showing what is the probable expectation of
life at different ages of males and females, and to some
extent we know how much that " expectation " differs
in different classes and sections of the population. The
actuaries at this present date, namely, 1922, argue from
the collected returns of births and of deaths at successive
ages that in England a newborn male child may legiti-
mately " expect " to live fifty-two years ; having reached
20, he may expect forty-five more years of life ; at 40
the " expectation " is twenty-eight; at 60, nearly fourteen ;
at 70, only eight and a half; at 90, more than two ; and
even at 100 yet one year more ! Women have a slightly
better prospect of long life than men. Thus, at 60 years
of age they have an expectation of fifteen and a half
instead of fourteen years. It is found that married
people have a prospect of somewhat longer life than
unmarried. It not only (as some people say) seems, but
actually is, longer. It appears from such statistics as
have been gathered that agricultural labourers in rural

[1] It must be remembered that the figures given by such tables are
not precisely the same to-day as they were forty years ago. The
conditions have improved, and the statistics now show a small but
marked increase in the " expectation of life " at various ages, though
the expectation at 55 years of age and after remains as it was. The
details of these important developments are discussed and brought
up to date in the periodic reports of the Registrar-General—so far as
this country is concerned. Those who desire to inspect the actual
figures and to trace the improvement in successive decades from the
year 1844 onwards can do so by consulting the "Annual Report of
the Chief Medical Officer. of the Ministry of Health (Sir George
Newman) for the year 1921," to be purchased through any bookseller
—price 1s. 6d. Life is twelve years longer to the newborn child than
it was in the days of our grandfathers. The general death-rate has
fallen from 21·4 per thousand in 1871–80 to 12·1 per thousand in 1921,
and the deaths of children under one year of age fell in the same period
from 149 to the astonishingly small figure of 83.

districts have at 60 the best prospects of long life of any class—three or four years better than the general population ; females of the aristocracy come next ; whilst business clerks are more than a year below the common figure. Distinguished people have somewhat shorter lives than undistinguished people ; they have to pay for their success.

We also know by the collection of facts at the census made in this country every ten years, and by the publication of the register of deaths, what is the extreme limit of age to which, as a matter of repute, any man or woman has attained in this country during the last fifty years or so. The mere statement by an individual, or by his or her friends, that he or she is of an unusual age, something over 100 years, is, of course, not sufficient evidence that such an age has actually been attained. There may be mistakes, lapse of memory, confusion of an old person with his or her father or mother. Consequently, before any statement of reputed great age is accepted as probably true, it is necessary to find the register of the birth of the supposed centenarian, and to obtain evidence that the birth-register really refers to the individual for whom exceptionally great age is claimed. Formerly this was a difficult, often an impossible, task, for two reasons : first, because the population in country places was less educated than is now the case, and therefore less accurate, less persuaded of the value of accuracy, and more given to indulgence in harmless flights of fancy ; and secondly, because the registers were only those of baptism or of a private, unofficial character and badly kept, if kept at all. Now, however, in Western Europe, it is less usual to meet with baseless declarations of excessive age on the part of old people. On the other hand, in Russia (before the war) and elsewhere, where the population is in a primitive stage of mental development, such assertions continued to be common, and were entered without verification for what they were worth (which was next to nothing) in official returns. According to the latter, one person in every 1000 born in Russia attains the age of 100 years!

In the middle of last century Sir George Cornewall Lewis exposed the loose conclusions which were then general as to the occurrence of cases in which man's life was prolonged to over 100 years, even to 130 or 150. He asked, according to correct scientific method, in each case what was the evidence for the assertion that the supposed marvel of longevity had attained the prodigious age attributed to him. "How is it," he said, "that people come to make these assertions?" There are many possible answers to this question, e.g. deliberate lying, ignorance, lapse of memory, genuine confusion of son with father, and also there is the possibility that the statement is made because it is true. The method pursued by Sir George Cornewall Lewis is the reasonable one to use in the investigation of all such assertions of marvellous occurrences. It is one which every one should apply to assertions as to the " rappings " and other " manifestations " of supposed disembodied spirits and as to asserted " second sight " or telepathy, and other statements by individuals that they have had experience of what are called " occult " agencies. The question to be put and answered in regard to all such assertions is not " Is this possible? " but " How is it that such and such persons come to make this assertion of their belief in, or supposed experience of, this improbable occurrence? " Sir G. C. Lewis showed that there was no evidence worthy of the name to support the traditions still generally accepted seventy years ago of the attainment of the great age of 130 to 150 years by Jenkins, Parr, and the Countess of Desmond. He even failed to find evidence of anyone completing a century of life, and accordingly held that no such case had occurred. The publication of his inquiries led, however, to the production by other investigators of evidence which satisfied him as to the existence of several instances in which the age of 100 years had been attained, and of some in which 103 years had been reached. Plenty of well-sifted and established cases of a longevity extending to this limit are now on record and undisputed, but I only know of one case in which there is plausible evidence that as much as 107 years was reached, and, so far as I am aware, that evidence has not been thoroughly examined and tested.

Under these circumstances I was, twenty years ago, not a little surprised to find the genial gossip of a respected weekly paper—I refrain from giving his name, as I am far from wishing to attack him in any way—writing : " Human vitality has increased. We are not far from the time when 200 instead of 100 will be looked upon as extreme old age." " Look at the evidence in favour of it," he says. " At the beginning of the year 1901, twenty survivors from the eighteenth century were alive in England." The oldest was born in 1793 and one in 1797. This does not, it is evident, take us far into a second century, nor is there anything novel or improbable about such a proportion of centenarians. So he proceeds to give some instances, by name, of much greater age, of the reality of which, however, there is no evidence worthy of attention, and none whatever offered by my friend the writer. The first is a Mr. Robert Tylor, said to have been the oldest postmaster in the country, who is reputed to have died in the year 1898 at the age of 134. Did he ? Another is Peter Bryan, of Tynan, who " cut a new set

of teeth at the age of 117 "—a proceeding which has
often been attributed to old people, and equally often the
belief in its occurrence has been shown to be due to faulty
observation.   No case of an aged individual cutting a
new tooth is admitted by those who are experts in
dentistry.   The jaw sometimes shrinks in old age and
exposes the stump of an old tooth previously concealed,
which is erroneously regarded as a " new " tooth.   Then
my friend cites Paul Czortan, of Temesover, in Hungary,
who, he declares without more ado, died in 1724 at the
age of 185, leaving a son aged 158.   With equal abrupt-
ness and apparent confidence he asserts that there was
once a man named Thomas Carew who lived to be 207
years old.   These are samples of those bald assertions of
" marvels of longevity," entirely devoid of any evidence
in their support, which Sir G. C. Lewis rightly declared to
be worthless.   It makes one rub one's eyes when one sees
them trotted out once more, after seventy years in the dust-
bin, by a writer who is not habitually reckless.   He goes
on to say that it is not work that ages, but leaving off
work.   The facts point, in my judgment, to the opposite
conclusion.   And he ends by expressing the opinion that
the " allotted span " of human life is being gradually
increased from threescore and ten to a much higher
figure, and states that " certain scientists " (certain or
uncertain ?) tell us that even tenscore will one day be
possible.   I am sorry to say that those prophetic scientists
are unknown to me.

What I find interesting in the views put forward by
the writer above cited is the notion that there is an
allotted span to human life—that which has been called a
" lease of life."   One might, on the contrary, conceive of
human life (or that of any animal or plant) as having no
inherent inborn limitation.   One might admit that it is

liable to be stopped by disease or violence at any time, or, on the other hand, finally arrested by the gradually accumulated effects of wear and tear resulting from years of struggle and disappointment. So that if the wear and tear were avoided or reduced to a minimum, human life might go on indefinitely. The view, however, that there is a lease of life, that the living organism is " wound up " for a certain limited " run," or, to put it in another way, that there is " a matter of life "—like the magical *peau de chagrin* of Balzac—which is gradually but surely used up by every vital act—is generally accepted as the true conception, at any rate in regard to the life of man and higher animals. " We live at the expense of our strength "—" *ex viribus vivimus,*" said Galen. In 1870 I published a little book on " Comparative Longevity," in which these matters are discussed. In later years Weismann, and also Metchnikoff, have dealt with the subject in valuable treatises, of which I will write further.

CHAPTER XX

LONGEVITY

AN important consideration in coming to any conclusion as to the probable extension of the duration of human life in the future or in the past,
beyond the limit of 100 years (to which in very exceptional
cases two or three additional years may be added), is as
to whether there is in the substance of living things an
innate, inherent limit of endurance, what has been called
" a lease of life." The view has been very generally
accepted that there is such a limit in most animals and
plants, if not in all. The conception may be illustrated
by the analogy of a clock, wound up to go for so many
days or weeks. It may be stopped by any one of a variety
of external agencies before the limit is reached, but by
no possible contingency can it continue " to go " beyond
the limit absolutely imposed by the mechanism wound up
to its fullest extent. Another analogy is that of an initial
provision to every individual of a certain limited amount
of material, which is very gradually but constantly and
inevitably used up in the mere process of living, and must
come to an end after the lapse of a period of time pro-
portional to the amount of the initial provision, whatever
care may be taken to avoid accidents and the waste or
injury to the inborn " matter of life." Whilst higher
animals have been regarded as possessing this limited
provision — this lease of life, varying in amount in

different species—it has been supposed that some lower animals are not so limited, but die only by the accident of violence or disease, or by growing so large that it becomes impossible for them to obtain the food necessary to maintain life, since ten smaller and younger individuals of the same species will be necessarily more capable of securing a sufficient quantity of scattered food in a given time than will be one individual equal in bulk to the ten small ones.

The notion that there is an inherent limit of life in animals—inherent necessary death due after a fixed lapse of time—is favoured by the obvious fact that there is a limit to the growth or increase of size of most animals and plants which are familiar to us—a limit which differs very greatly in different species. It is held that just as we cannot by taking thought add a cubit to our stature, so we cannot by taking thought add ten years to our " lease of life," though there may be born " giants of longevity " as there are born " giants of stature." I have, many years ago, written of this lease of life as " potential longevity." It is, however, an elusive quantity. For it is admitted that in wild animals, as well as in man, the actual cessation of life must be determined in every individual case, not only by this innate or specific potential longevity—differing in every species but common to all the individuals of a species — but also by the results of the daily necessary " wear and tear," injuries and diseases to which all the individuals of a species are naturally exposed—causes which are external to and apart from the living substance itself. There is an average of such injurious incidents in the natural life of every species of living thing. The " recuperative " power of the organism to a large extent removes the injurious results of these destructive external agencies, but, like proverbial drops of water, they in the long run tell. Like the equally proverbial pitcher carried to the well, the animal or plant, sooner or later—after a lapse of time which has an average value for each distinct species according to those natural circumstances to which it is adapted—encounters one or a series of injuries which weaken it and finally cause its death, whatever its inherent lease of life or specific potential longevity may be.

It is difficult, if not impossible, to separate the animal (or even man) from these contingent external injurious agencies, and to guard it under observation so as to determine what is the amount of its absolute potential longevity. We really know very little of the length of life of animals in their wild, natural conditions. Of the longevity of those which live in deep waters or are, for various other reasons, inaccessible to constant observation, we can only form rough guesses. It is easier in the case of plants of all kinds, herbs, shrubs, and trees, to arrive at the facts, because plants do not shrink from man's approach.

Most of our knowledge of the longevity of animals is derived from the observation of them in non-natural conditions, either when protected by man from their natural enemies, or bred as domesticated animals. The length of life which is the result of an animal's or plant's innate lease of life, its specific potential longevity, when checked and diminished by the operation of the injurious agencies which inevitably belong to its native conditions of life as a wild animal, can be estimated in some cases. It must be recognized by a distinct term, and may be called " the effective longevity of a species," the longevity which is the regular average performance of those members of a species which reach maturity, the outcome of their innate hereditary lease of life, subjected to the operation of injurious agencies, which are a normal and necessary accompaniment of the natural course of life proper to the species.

Some few facts as to this effective longevity may be cited. Dogs are " old " at twelve years ; they show " senile decay " (loss of teeth, etc.) at that age. In wild nature they die at that age, killed by carnivorous animals or by other younger animals of their own species, or by inability to capture food. Under man's care they may live to twice that age. Horses in the natural wild state die (by the wearing away of the teeth) at twenty years, but have been kept alive till thirty and even forty years when domesticated and provided with suitable food. The longevity of the elephant has been exaggerated ; probably its habitual wild life does not exceed fifty years. Bovines, goats, deer, and sheep probably do not live more than from twelve to fifteen years in wild conditions. The rabbit and the guinea-pig and mammals of this size have an effective longevity, in the wild state, of six or seven years. The lion and tiger probably live some fifteen years in wild conditions, and may be kept to twice that age by human care. The cat has in the wild state a life of eight or nine years ; it has been kept by man to eighteen years of age. We really know nothing of the habitual length of life of the great apes. Birds certainly live longer than do mammals of similar bulk. Geese, swans, ravens, and some birds of prey have been known to reach the age of fifty years ; even canaries (in cages) may live to twenty years of age. Many well-certified cases of parrots and cockatoos reaching the age of eighty years and more are known. Crocodiles and tortoises have apparently great length of life—some kept in tanks or gardens are supposed, on good grounds, to be 200 years old. Some fish, like pike and carp, kept under observation in ponds, appear to have exceeded 150 years in age—though the evidence is not conclusive. It has been supposed that reptiles and fish, which often continue to grow as long as they live, have not—as mammals and birds are supposed to have—a limited " lease of life." As we shall see, it is, as a matter of fact, a difficult thing to arrive at a conclusion as to the presence or the absence of this " lease of life " in any group of animals. Most of the smaller invertebrates are shortlived. Insects live from a year to seventeen years in the larval state, but have as a rule only a few hours to six months in the perfect or " imago " state. Some molluscs are shown by their size and that of their shells to live twenty years at least, but most have only from two to a dozen years of life. The larger crustacea (such as the lobster and big crabs) may be inferred from their size to have twenty or more years of life : smaller forms die when a year old. The most interesting fact known about length of life in one of the lower animals is this, namely, that a common sea-anemone (Actinia mesembryanthemum), captured by Sir John Dalzell in 1828, lived in a tank in Edinburgh for sixty years, and produced many hundred young ones during that period. The eventual cause of its death is not known, but was apparently some mischance, and not senile decay.

Trees of various kinds have different effective longevities. Thus fruit trees and trees with soft wood, such as the poplar and the willow, live from fifty to sixty years. They are usually killed in the end by destructive fungi and moulds. The cypress and the olive are said to live 800 years, the oak 1500, the elm 300, the cedar 2000, the yew 3000, and the big Californian trees 4000 years, but all these figures are probably greatly exaggerated.

A new aspect is given to the problem of longevity when we inquire into the case of the simplest living things, those unicellular organisms consisting of a single nucleated droplet of living protoplasm, such as the Amœbæ, the Infusoria, the unicellular Algæ, and the Bacteria. They have no limit of life, no senility. They keep on multiplying by fission, and careful observations show that the same stock may be kept and carried on, nourishing itself, growing, and dividing, for an indefinite time. They show no signs of age provided that food is present ; they seem to be practically immortal unless accident of some kind checks their career. They justify the view that living substance or protoplasm does not necessarily as a result of its chemical and physical constitution undergo natural decay and death. This has led Weismann to point out that in every many-celled animal and plant there are some such immortal protoplasmic cells, the germ-cells, or reproductive cells. They arise in each new individual by a setting aside of some of the cells which result from the division of the parental egg-cell, and whilst the other cells which form the body which moves and feeds and assumes characteristic form, naturally die in the course of time and disappear, the germ-cells or some of them persist, giving rise (as egg-cells or germ-cells) to new individuals and to new germ-cells. Thus it is the body-cells which die as a sort of " husk " which has served its turn and protected the germ-cells until they are set free to multiply and start a new individual or husk, enclosing in its turn a certain number of cells of the immortal germ-plasm.

From this point of view it would appear that the greater or less duration or longevity of the body enclosing the deathless germ-plasm is a question of physiological adaptation which is varied, according to the advantage of

the species, by natural selection.   In some organisms it
is an advantage that the body-husk should get quickly
through its business, and be replaced by a new generation ;
in others a long duration of the body once grown to full
size and complexity is advantageous for the preservation
of the species.   The suggestion here is that the potential
length of life of the body (as apart from the germ-cells) is
an hereditary character of every species, increased or
diminished by the natural selection of variations in that
character, as are other characters, in consequence of the
struggle for existence and the survival of the fittest
variations.   This conception involves the supposition
that there is in multicellular animals an ultimate innate
tendency of the body-cells (as distinct from the reproductive cells) to senile decay and death, which may be
remote or may come on rapidly.   And there is no reason
for rejecting the supposition that some of the products of
division of immortal " cells " of protoplasm, themselves
incapable of death by old age, should acquire this
mortality, this quality of senescence, and ultimate natural
death, as a secondary and definite character of the body
or envelope which is formed as the carrier of the new
germ-cells.

Metchnikoff, on the other hand, who fifteen years ago
wrote a most interesting book on this subject (" The
Nature of Man " : London, Heinemann), avoids, as far
as possible, the assumption that there is, in any kind of
plants or animals, an inherent innate limit of life.   He
devotes his attention to the examination of the nature
of that enfeeblement which comes on in old age in most
living things, that diseased or unhealthy state to which
we have already had to refer as " senility " or " senile
decay," and he is led to the conclusion that though in
some cases (such as that of the insects known as " day-

flies ") there is evidence of a strictly limited innate " potential longevity," yet that in higher animals there is no need to assume any such inherent limit to the lease of life. The changes due to disease and external injurious agencies are (according to Metchnikoff) sufficient to account for the stoppage of life, and if we could avoid all those injurious agencies, as we can and do avoid many of them (but not so many as we might), human life and the life of animals similarly protected and directed by man might be longer as a rule than it is, and far happier and healthier in its later years. The result to be aimed at, according to Metchnikoff, is not that of increasing the extreme limit of life from 100 to 150 or 200 years, but that of raising the general length of life to be expected by men and women of 30 years of age, so that instead of dying as a rule at or before 65 years of age, they may as a rule survive to 100 years. Simultaneously the last thirty or forty years of that lengthened life would become a contented and healthy period instead of being marked by labour and sorrow. It is a noteworthy fact that whilst the records of the Registrar-General, extending over more than half a century, above cited, show a continuous diminution of the death-rate in mankind below the age of fifty-five, there is no similar evidence of any corresponding increase in the number of years to which life is likely to extend once the age of fifty-five has been attained.

CHAPTER XXI

METCHNIKOFF ON OLD AGE

WHATEVER may be the causes at work—whether the exhaustion by the efflux of time of an initial limited power of endurance, or, on the other hand, the cumulative result of wear and tear and disease acting on living substance, which has in itself no inherent tendency to " play out " or " run down " after any length of living—we have the important fact that the " May of life " after a certain length of time does, as a rule, " fall into the sear, the yellow leaf," and gives place to " senile decay." Metchnikoff (in his book called " The Nature of Man ") has made a special study of this " senile decay." He has no difficulty in showing that in man and the higher animals, as well as many of the lower animals, this senile decay asserts itself after a certain period of life. It is a condition of injurious change and enfeeblement in the tissues of the body which has not been sufficiently studied by modern methods, but which must be so studied with the view of averting it in mankind. Metchnikoff seems to doubt the existence in man of a necessary or natural inherent tendency to this decay, but he cites the life-history of many insects, in which, as in some other animals, he admits the existence of a sharp and inherent limit to life. A familiar case is that of the Day-flies (Ephemerids), which, after spending two or three years as " larvæ " under water in the mud of streams, feeding voraciously, undergo a rapid change and become winged insects which fly in huge numbers over the water. Their flight lasts only an hour or two, and is occupied in the fertilization of the eggs, after which they fall dead or dying into the water.   They have no jaws and cannot feed, but they do not die from want of food, nor from the exhaustion due to the passage of the reproductive material from their bodies.   Metchnikoff has examined many such dead individuals carefully, and found that among them were many males which had not discharged their sperm. He also satisfied himself that death was not due to any deadly microbe which suddenly attacks the flies as an epidemic.   It seems practically certain that they die simply because they are, when they escape into the air as " flies," only " wound up " for about six hours' further activity—a short lease of life which no experimental ingenuity on the part of man can prolong.   A curious and important fact is that these insects (as also the winged form of ants and the little green-flies or plant-lice) show no fear or shrinking from being caught and handled. They have lost the instinct of self-preservation, though when in the larval condition and living in water they are difficult to catch, and run away with great activity from a tube with which one endeavours to pick them up from the jar of water in which one is keeping them for observation.   There is apparently an " instinct " for life in most animals, and also in some animals, when old age has arrived, an instinct for death—a willing surrender and abandonment of the struggle.

I confess that whilst I hold with Metchnikoff that the avoidable diseases and " wearing " away of parts of the body are accountable for the pains and usual discomfort of old age and, as a rule, for eventual death, so that we cannot, with regard to man and higher animals, determine with accuracy the existence of cases of "natural death" from inherent limitation of the power of endurance of the protoplasm or living substance of the body, yet it seems to me most probable that there is such a limitation, more remote in large animals than in smaller ones, and less remote in those which exhibit a greater activity or "output" in their lives than in those which are less active, and live, so to speak, more slowly.

Whatever view may be considered probable in regard to the existence of a natural limit to possible life in man, there can be no doubt as to the vast importance of the facts and views put forward by Metchnikoff as to the power which we possess, by the acquirement and application of accurate knowledge, to lessen or altogether avert those changes in the tissues which make old age miserable and cause death at an earlier period than is absolutely necessary. Mankind have no liking for old age, and yet, even when old, retain their instinctive dread and aversion for death. A distinguished physiologist (Longet) has written : " The old feel that their task in life is accomplished and believe themselves to be universally grudged the space they occupy in the world. This renders them suspicious of all around them and jealous of the young. Their craving for solitude and the uncertainty of their tempers are due to the same cause. All old people are not like this, of course. The hearts of some remain youthful and beat strongly within their feeble frames. . . . The years speed onward, every round of the clock bringing the end nearer, and every hour adding a new wrinkle to their faces, some fresh weakness and some new regret. Their bodies become decrepit ; their backbones, too weak to hold them upright, curve over, and bend them downwards towards the earth."

Metchnikoff inquires as to what precisely are the changes which bring about this state of things. It is a remarkable fact that, in spite of the misery of old age, old people cling to life. The result of the examination of a large number of cases is that, with the rarest exceptions, even very old people desire to go on living. Metchnikoff thinks that this is due partly to the dread of death and " the something after death " which is instilled from their earliest years into nearly all races and populations, but that it is also partly due to a feeling on the part of old people that something is still due to them, that they have not had their fair share of happiness, and that even in their latest years " something will turn up." If old age could be made healthy, if the diseases which break down healthy life, before its natural limit, could be averted, and men could, without any sense of misfortune or injustice, end their lives, without prolonged decay and suffering, by " natural death " or mere " cessation of living," as do the day-flies, that natural end would be accompanied by an " instinct for death " like the " instinct for sleep " at the end of a long and happy day. Tokarski, a Russian writer, gives us the words of an old woman who had lived a hundred years. She is one of the rare cases known of glad acquiescence in the natural termination of life. She said : " If you come to live as long as I have lived, you will understand not only that it is possible not to fear death, but to feel the same need for death as for sleep."

Philosophy and religion have in vain endeavoured, in all past ages of civilization, to fortify and to comfort man in bearing the pains and disappointments of old age and the inevitable death to which it leads—not desired, not welcomed as release and rest, but usually feared, and often not only feared but resented. The promise of a happy future after death is what the Christian Church has offered as compensation for the unmerited sufferings of this life. On the other hand, Science has from its earliest days been busy in the attempt to so regulate human life as to avert the sufferings of men in this world and to correct the " disharmonies " of human life—that imperfect adjustment of the structure and living processes of man to the natural conditions in which he finds himself. Man lives in a state of warfare and struggle with natural conditions to which he has been brought by the sudden and unparalleled development of his intelligence, and by his evasion of those methods of " destruction of the unfit " by which Nature had maintained on the earth's surface a happy, healthy population of animals and plants for countless ages before man's emergence. The parable of the tree of knowledge in the garden of Eden is the recognition of this truth, and it is emphasized in the words of a great Hebrew of ancient days : " In much wisdom is much grief ; and he that increaseth knowledge increaseth sorrow." It is the business of science to take men beyond this phase of imperfect knowledge. Much knowledge leads, and has led, to much grief, but greater knowledge—greater far than the old writer dreamed of—will, we can clearly see, destroy sorrow and bring man to ever-growing happiness—and is even now doing so ! Metchnikoff declares—and in my judgment he is right—that full and complete knowledge of the causes of decay in old age can be arrived at (though it will take many generations to obtain it), and that such knowledge will enable man deliberately to prevent that decay, so that the ideal of human life shall be realized, namely, the completion by all men of the normal cycle of healthy life, rounded off by natural death as by a sleep. Our object and our expectation should not be to extend the term of human life beyond its present natural limit, which appears to be about 100 years, but to make it the regular and easy thing for every one to reach that age and to be healthy and useful (since the experience and wisdom of the old is valuable) until the last.

What, then, are the obstacles to this general extension of life to the end of a healthy (and therefore happy) second half-century ?   They are, firstly, the wearing out of the teeth ; and, secondly, the hardening of the arteries and changes similar to that process.   The higher animals —the hairy warm-blooded quadrupeds—which have survived the dangers of youth and reached maturity— come, as a rule, to their death by the wearing out of their teeth.   Wolves, lions, tigers, bears, and cats, in wild nature, wear down and lose their teeth.   When toothless they cannot catch their prey nor protect themselves in competition with their fellows.   They become enfeebled by insufficiency of food, and die from consequent disease or from the attacks of their younger rivals.   The same is true of herbivorous animals—horses, bovines, sheep, and deer.   Their teeth wear out.   The same is true of the apes, and was true of primitive man.   But at an early period of his development man learnt to select, to prepare, and to soften food, so that the failure of his teeth was not so serious a loss to him as to other animals.   Later he provided himself in old age with artificial teeth, and so the loss of his natural teeth ceased to be a cause of death.

But those serious changes which are exhibited in their most obvious form in the hardening of the arteries in old age still remain to be discussed.   The various living cells and the tissues which they build up in the human body are divided by Metchnikoff into (a) the less delicate or more resistant and permanent tissues, and (b) the more special delicate tissues which he terms the "nobler." The latter are, in the first place, the immensely important nerve-cells of the brain and spinal cord, which are never multiplied in adult life nor replaced when injured or destroyed. Further, we have in this category the gland-cells, such as those of the kidney and liver, and the contractile muscular cells, which, though capable of repair and new growth, are yet delicate and highly sensitive to unhealthy chemical conditions (poisons). The permanent, resistant, and exuberant tissues (which Metchnikoff points to as the "baser" or "non-noble") are the fibrous skeleton-making or enveloping tissues which are spread everywhere through the body as a wonderfully subdivided penetrating framework in all the minutest, as well as the largest, parts or architectural units of our structure. With them, and originating from them, are found the motile, often floating, protoplasmic "eater-cells" or "phagocytes" (see Chapter VI), which devour (as does the unicellular animalcule, the amœba) all intrusive bacteria, and all the dead or enfeebled bits of the complex animal body. The hardening of arteries, the destruction of kidney-cells and brain-cells, which goes on in old people, is due to the relatively too great activity of this fibre-forming tissue, and of the "eater-cells," which destroy and devour the nobler cells, and fill up their place by base fibrous, or (as it is called) "connective" tissue—mere "packing," devoid of the special qualities of the tissues which it replaces. Thus the elastic resilient arteries become hardened, the great glands (such as kidney and liver) largely replaced by inert "stuffing," and the brain similarly deteriorated. Even the loss of colour in the hair is shown by Metchnikoff to be due to "eater-cells," which in old age enter the individual hairs and eat up, engulf, and dissolve the pigment granules.

The problem, therefore, is how to arrest this relatively excessive activity of the connective tissue and eater-cells. And to arrive at an answer to this question we must find out what it is which leads to their increased and destructive activity, and then endeavour to find a means of removing that cause ; or, on the other hand, of increasing the resistance and relative strength of the nobler tissue-cells. This is necessarily a long and elaborate inquiry. But the following facts are established. The enfeeblement of the nobler contractile cells of the walls of arteries, and their replacement by " stuffing," as well as the similar changes in the brain and in the great glands are favoured by certain poisons which man habitually takes into his body. The first is universally recognized to be alcohol ; the second is the poison of " syphilis," that insidious infectious disease which is so widely spread and is caused by the excessively minute microbe discovered by Schaudin and named by him, Treponema pallidum ; the third is the poison absorbed from the mass of putrefying unabsorbed food which fills the large intestine of man. The action of these three poisons is to paralyse and weaken the nobler tissue-cells. They are more or less successfully resisted by the younger and more vigorous section of the human population ; but their efforts accumulate. After middle age the results of their injurious work become more and more obvious and increased in actual amount and proportion, producing the enfeeblement and decay which we associate with old age.

The indulgence in alcoholic drinks is a cause which we can at once remove or reduce to a minimum. The widespread disease syphilis we can, easily and readily, extirpate, if and when Governments decide so to do. It has been shown that 45 per cent or nearly half the deaths from arterial sclerosis or hardening of

the arteries are due to these two causes—alcoholism and
syphilis.   Rheumatism and gout only play a small part
in setting up hardening of the arteries.   It is held to be
highly probable that the poisons fabricated by the mass
of microbes congregated in the human intestine—that
part of it called the large intestine—are responsible
for the rest of the arterial hardening, which (do not
let us forget) is the characteristic feature of senile
decay.   We have now to see how this cause can be
removed.

We have seen that the too great indulgence in alcohol
together with a widespread infectious disease are the chief
causes (in youth and middle age) of that poisoning of the
nobler tissues which results in the hardening of the arteries
and the replacement of important " nobler " tissues by
fibrous packing or connective tissue, and thus to that
decay and enfeeblement which marks the old age of man.
These causes are under our control.   A third cause,
according to Metchnikoff, is the poisoning of the tissues
by products manufactured by microbes in the large
intestine and absorbed into the blood.   The grounds for
this conclusion and the ways in which this cause of senile
decay may be avoided remain for consideration.

An old and accepted saying is : " A man is as old as
his arteries."   It points to the fact not only that the
hardening of the walls of the arteries is itself destructive
of health and dangerous to life, but that similar changes
in other parts besides the walls of the arteries are going
on at the same time.   If we could prevent the poisoning
of the body by the products of intestinal microbes, in
addition to avoiding excess in the use of alcohol and
infection by the Treponema microbe—two precautions
which are assuredly within our power—we should in all

probability be able to ensure for mankind a healthy and happy old age.

The human intestine contains an enormous quantity of bacteria which, according to the researches of the eminent biologist, Strassburger, increase at the rate of 128 million millions a day. That gives some indication of the gigantic number present. They are not all of one kind, but comprise an enormous variety, some of which are more abundant than others. One-third part of the human excreta consists of these bacteria! There are but few, relatively, in the active digesting portion of the alimentary canal. By far the greater number are lodged in the terminal or lower part of the intestine, which is called the " large intestine " or " colon," and is in man without action as a digestive organ. This is a very wide but short portion of the intestine, as broad as three fingers, and only from 5 to 6 feet in length. It is disposed as an ascending, a transverse, and a descending portion, the last ending in the rectum and the vent. The food, before it reaches the " large intestine," has passed through the œsophagus 10 inches long, the stomach—a pear-shaped sac holding 5 pints and about 10 inches long—and the small intestine, which is from 25 to 30 feet long. This part of the intestine is called " small " because it is a narrow tube little more than an inch broad, disposed or packed within the abdomen in undulating coils and convolutions. It joins the much wider but short " large intestine " just within the right edge of the bony hip or pelvic basin. Here is situated, at the commencement of the large intestine, the curious little sac, " the cæcum," with its wormlike blind process—the " vermiform appendix "—which so often becomes diseased and has to be removed by the surgeon. The whole of the digestive process of man takes place in the stomach and in the 25 feet of small intestine ; none in the cæcum nor in the large intestine.   The cæcum, or blind sac, and the 6 feet of large intestine are quite useless.   No digestion goes on in them ; but the remains of the food passing into them putrefy under the action of the enormous population of bacteria.

The products of the putrefaction produced by some (though not all) of the kinds of bacteria usually present in man's large intestine are definite poisons.   These poisons (phenol and indol) have been identified by physiological chemists and followed after their absorption into the blood.   They are eventually passed out of the body by the kidneys.   In healthy, vigorous people they are not produced in sufficient quantity to do much harm. But it is owing to their production that constipation has such injurious results, and in all persons of sedentary habits, or those in whom the intestine is weakened and does not rapidly empty itself, very serious disturbances— headache, lassitude, and even poisoning of the brain (mania)—are the consequence of their formation.   There seems to be sufficient experimental ground for concluding that these poisons when absorbed act upon the " nobler " tissues so as to enfeeble them and stimulate the eater-cells to activity and to the destruction of the nobler cells and their replacement by useless, inert, fibrous, connective tissues.[1]

Here, then, we find present in man a wide, capacious tract of intestine which is not only of no use to him, but a seat of positive and serious danger.   How has this come about ?   In flesh-eating animals this last portion of intestine—the so-called large intestine or " colon "—

[1] It is nevertheless true that further observation and experiment are needed in order to establish this conclusion with certainty.

is absent.   Dogs, cats, lions, and such animals have not
got it.   It is of no use in the digestion of animal food
(flesh, etc.).   But in the grass-eating, leaf-eating, and
fruit-eating animals—cattle, sheep, horses, rabbits, many
monkeys—the colon and cæcum, constituting the " large
intestine," are of full size, and assist in digestion.   The
woody material (cellulose) present in vegetable food is
acted upon by the bacteria which accumulate in the large
intestine of herbivorous animals, and this substance,
which cannot be digested by the juices of the stomach
and small intestine, is altered or " fermented " by the
bacteria in such a way as to produce not poisons, but
valuable nutritive material, which is absorbed by the
animal and nourishes it.   An interesting suggestion as to
the further advantage to herbivorous animals of the
distended capacious large intestine is put forward by
Metchnikoff.   These animals have to run for their lives
when pursued by carnivorous enemies.   The large
intestine enables them to retain their partly digested food
for a longer time than can an animal which has no large
intestine.   They are not delayed in their flight by stop-
ping to empty the bowel, and, moreover, they are able to
continue the digestion of the woody vegetable materials
retained in them when they have reached a position of
safety and repose.   Man, it seems, has inherited his
large intestine from vegetarian ancestors even more
remote than the apes, and though he has changed his
habits as to food and has benefited by giving up woody
fibre and by feeding on the succulent parts of plants and
the prepared flesh of animals, yet the desirable change in
his bodily structure corresponding to his change of food
has not followed.

The large intestine is one of the many instances of
" disharmony " between the more recently acquired

habits or mode of life of an organism and its ancient inherited structure, whether this be structure of other organs or of the brain and nervous system exhibited in instincts. It has long been recognized that in man there are many such delays (for so we may consider them) in the adjustment of this or that part of his mechanism to the new conditions to which, on the whole, he has become successfully adapted so as to flourish and spread over the whole surface of the world. The useless " wisdom teeth "—clearly on the way to disappear altogether—are an instance. They are not only useless, but are seats of disease, sometimes causing death. The gaps in the fibrous wall of the abdomen which were harmless in man's four-footed ancestors, and even in arboreal apes, are a danger to man now that he has taken to the upright pose in walking and running. They permit in the upright, but not in the more horizontal, attitude the painful and dangerous extrusions of loops of intestine through the abdominal wall known as " hernia." This is a " disharmony," a want of adaptation of man's structure in one particular respect to the upright carriage, although great and important adaptations to it in very many other respects (such as the structure of the leg and the foot, vertebral column, balance of the head, etc.) have been perfected.

Can man then step in and himself " artificially " bring about the disappearance of the " disharmony " of his intestinal structure, so as to avoid poisoning himself by putrefactive bacteria ? He has already in various ways undertaken a certain amount of such carving and remodelling of his own structure. The dwindled cæcum and its wormlike termination are naturally, but slowly, on their way to disappearance. In the horse and the rabbit they are of twenty times the size, relatively to the rest of the body, which they present in man. Surgeons now remove from man the dwindled piece which is the most dangerous on account of its liability to ulceration and abscess, namely, the wormlike appendix. Not only that, but (in, it is true, a much smaller number of cases) the whole of the large intestine has in recent years been removed from patients because its diseased state had led to excessive absorption of putrefactive poison from its contents. A considerable number of persons are alive and well who have undergone this operation, and are all the better for having no large intestine ! Though, as Metchnikoff says, we cannot expect, in spite of the progress of surgery, to see in our time the large intestine removed by operation as a usual thing, yet perhaps, in the distant future, such a proceeding will become the rule.

Failing this remedy, there remain to us two procedures in order to preserve humanity against the senile decay due to the poisons produced by certain putrefactions of the contents of the large intestine. The first is to control the intestinal flora—the flora of bacteria—so as to exclude from the large intestine the poison-producing kind, which gets " sown " or carried into it inevitably with the raw food we swallow ; the second is to inject into the blood and tissues " serums " prepared, as we now can see our way to prepare them, so that they shall have the property either of strengthening and encouraging the resistance of the nobler tissue-cells, those of brain, glands, and muscles, or, on the other hand, have the property of holding in check the phagocytes and the fibre-forming tissues so as to restrain the undesirable invasion and multiplication by them in highly developed organs.

The problem of controlling our intestinal " gardens,"

and cultivating there what bacteria we choose, and destroying or weeding out those we discover to be harmful, has advanced further towards solution than has the problem of preparing the serums suggested. A very simple fact in regard to the bacteria comes to our aid. It is this. Some bacteria will grow only in an alkaline liquid, other kinds will only grow in an acid liquid. A slight predominance of alkaline or acid is sufficient. The bacterium which produces the " phenol-indol " poisons in the large intestine absolutely requires slightly alkaline surroundings. You have only to make the contents of the large intestine somewhat acid, and the poisonous " weed " is stopped, never again to flourish so long as the acid condition is maintained. It might be supposed that this end could be attained by the simple swallowing of acid fluids. But that is not so. It is not possible (without injury) to take sufficient quantities of acid to keep the large intestine's contents acid. Fortunately, there is a microbe—the lactic bacillus—which can, and does, grow in the large intestine (when encouraged to do so), and produces from sugar a very efficient acid, called " lactic acid." All we have to do then is to swallow the lactic bacillus and also suitable sugar in such quantity that they shall pass through all the thirty feet of the alimentary canal, and arrive in the large intestine, there to grow and suppress, by the production of acid, the acid-hating poisonous bacteria. Many races of men have—without consciously aiming at the repression of poison-producing bacteria—for ages carried out this procedure, feeding largely on " sour milk," which is milk turned acid by the lactic bacillus, which lives and swarms in the soured liquid. It has been found that there is no diffi-culty in taking every day such a quantity of " sour milk " and appropriate sugar as shall ensure the establishment of the acid-producing " lactic " bacillus in the large intestine of man. A vast number of persons in Europe and America, especially those who were suffering from the more obvious effects of the absorption of poison from the large intestine—have of late years adopted this " regime " with complete success. It has been found, definitely and precisely by chemical analysis, that persons who were passing the phenol-indol poisons through the kidney (having absorbed them from the large intestine), so soon as their large intestines become " planted " with the lactic organism, cease to absorb those poisons and to evacuate them through the kidneys. The poisons are no longer produced. The problem of cultivating one's own bacterial garden in the large intestine seems certainly to have been solved, and a definite step taken towards freeing our tissues of the poisons due to alkaline putre-faction in the large intestine, which are one of the chief causes of " senile decay."

As to the injection into the human body of serums designed to strengthen the higher or nobler elements of the organism and to weaken the aggressive capacity of the phagocytes or eater-cells, this method is suggested by Metchnikoff not as an actual but as a possible solution of the problem, worthy of consideration. Serums capable of poisoning particular kinds of cells have been prepared (by Dr. Bordet, of the Pasteur Institute) by taking samples of any one kind of cell—say, those of the liver or the kidney or the red blood corpuscles—from one species of animal A and injecting them alive and fresh into the blood vessels of another species of animal B. After several injections spread over some days, the blood serum of the animal operated on (B) becomes destructive or poisonous to the particular kind of cells taken from the animal (A). And this serum can now be injected into a living animal of the first species (A). It has been found

13

that such serums injected in large quantities into the animal species A destroy the kind of cells used in their preparation, but if injected in smaller quantities actually strengthen them.   The action is analogous to that of certain medicinal poisons which kill in large doses but in weak doses improve or strengthen the action of certain tissues.   Thus it seems quite possible to prepare a serum which, if injected into the human body, should strengthen a given kind of nobler or higher tissue, and another serum which should, when similarly used, poison and weaken the phagocytes and the fibre-forming invading worthless tissues.

It is, it seems to me, desirable thus briefly to place before the reader what are the possible lines of inquiry and experiment which present themselves to the investigator as likely to place in our hands the means of removing the worst features of the series of changes which we call " senile decay."   We have lived to see the old alchemists' dream of the transmutation of elements realized by the discovery of radium.   It is not impossible that a generation or two later than ours may witness the discovery of something not very unlike the " elixir vitæ," though not altogether as powerful as that mythical preparation was expected to be by those who in past ages sought for it. The attitude of modern science towards the future possibility of ameliorating old age and lengthening the healthy normal life of man is one of hope based on results already achieved.   But as to the future increase of man's tenure of life to a term beyond 100 years we have no positive indication.

Perhaps it is as well to note in conclusion that it is universally agreed that those who would enjoy a happy and prolonged old age must eat less, drink less, and smoke less, work less, and play less, than they did in the prime of life.   There must be a real and willing reduction in all these quantities in proportion to the diminished vigour of the individual.   He must also worry less and hurry less than was his habit, and he must never run the risk of doing a harmful thing, for his chance of escaping without permanent injury is no longer so good as it was !

CHAPTER XXII

GIANTS

IT is a reasonable suggestion that there is a similarity between the limitation in the quality of the living matter of many plants and animals which sets a term to their endurance or possible age, and that limitation which results in a cessation of growth in many kinds of organisms after a certain size has been attained. We recognize a certain size as that which is characteristic of man and of various species of wild animals, and we are accustomed to a certain small variation in that size, so that individuals are somewhat " shorter " or " taller." But any large divergence from the characteristic height (amounting in the case of man to a third more or less than the average or normal height) we regard as alto-gether exceptional, and speak of the abnormally tall individuals as " giants," and the abnormally short as " dwarfs." It is abundantly clear that the lease of life or potential longevity is not greater in giants nor less in dwarfs than in other men. Whilst the two things are independent of one another, it is yet the fact that there is both in relation to longevity and to stature, an innate limitation in very many species of animals as well as men. It is a legitimate supposition that the innate lease of life varies in individuals owing to an initial quality of the living material of the individual in much the same way as does the innate capacity for growth to a normal size or to a size less or greater than what is normal or usual in the species. And so there may be rare individuals born with exceptional innate longevity as there are rare individuals born with exceptional innate growth-power. Many cases have been recorded of human beings who have exhibited senile decay and died of it before attaining twenty years of age.

Perhaps all human beings who reach 100 years of age should be regarded as exceptional individuals, like giants. There do not appear to be many known instances of a giant exceeding the average stature of man by more than a half of the normal measurement. Frederick the Great's Scotch giant measured 8 ft. 3 in. in height. Patrick Cotler, an Irishman, who died at Clifton (Bristol) in 1802, was 8 ft. 7 in. high. The Irish giant, " O'Brien " (Charles Byrne), whose skeleton is preserved in the museum of the Royal College of Surgeons, was 8 ft. 4 in. in height. Chang or Chang-woo-goo, the Chinese giant, whom I saw several times in London in 1880, was 8 ft. 2 in. high, and a perfectly well-proportioned, good-looking man of charming manners. All these, however, were exceeded by Winkelmaier, an Austrian, who was exhibited in London in 1887, and was 8 ft. 9 in. in height. He, again, was exceeded by Machnow, a Russian, born at Charkow, whom I saw in Paris in 1905. He stood 9 ft. 3 in., and weighed 25 st. 10 lb. Machnow is the tallest giant of whom we have trustworthy record.

Very usually giants and dwarfs do not present the proportions of ordinary individuals magnified or diminished. A giant's head is smaller and a dwarf's head is larger than would be that of an average man magnified or diminished. Chang was an exception to this rule, and presented a near approach to the usual proportions of head, body, and limbs. Not infrequently great height is due to excessive length of the legs, the rest of the body not being of unusual size. And very frequently giants (especially those rare cases approaching or exceeding 8 ft. in height) are weak and unhealthy and die young. The record, on the other hand, of dwarfs who have reached adult age and been known as " celebrities " does not lead to the supposition that they are short-lived. Two feet in height appears to be about the limit of minuteness recorded for a healthy dwarf, and is very rare. Three feet is a good record for an adult dwarf. Charles Stratton, who exhibited himself under the name of " General Tom Thumb " from 1844 onwards, was 2 ft. 7 in. high when 25 years old.   He took £600 in the first week of his appearance on exhibition in London, whilst Haydon, the painter, who exhibited his picture, " The Banishment of Aristides," in the same building, drew but £7, 13s. The artist committed suicide. The dwarf married a diminutive lady in 1863, and died in comfortable retirement in 1883.

It is a noteworthy fact that both giants and dwarfs are the offspring of parents of normal height. On the other hand, there is a very general belief that longevity —that is, an abnormally long lease of life—runs in families. It is an example of the difficulty which is found in arriving at a well-founded conclusion in so many matters where inheritance of qualities or capacities is in question, that it is still doubtful whether the actual quality of potential long life is one which is transmitted from parents to offspring. The habits of life which we know are likely to favour long life are, we also know, likely to be transmitted, and, further, to be handed on by tradition and training.   Hence it is difficult in any family to attribute the attainment of an age exceeding 80 or 90 years on the part of many of its members to an inherent potential longevity inherited by all or most of the members of the family, rather than to the inheritance of traditions and character affecting the conduct of life and leading to avoidance of disease, and to moderation in eating, drinking, and those abuses of strength which shorten the lives of most men. On the other hand, there is no reason to doubt that the breeder of this or that kind of animal could produce a long-lived or a short-lived strain or race by the usual method of selection.

Giants have been the subject of exaggerated tradition and myth in early times, and wonderful stories of prehistoric men 15 feet and 20 feet high have been accepted even as late as a century ago, just as the tradition has been accepted of men living to be several hundred years old in those remote days, of which we have no contemporary records. The Greeks told of the Cyclopes and wild tribes of giants. "Giant legends" of the kind are common in Europe and Asia. The barbaric tribes who resisted the incursions of a more civilized race were described as big and stupid giants, and were exaggerated into monsters in the legends of their conquerors. Mere pictures and effigies of gigantic size have undoubtedly given rise to legends of the existence of giants. The misunderstanding of works of art has, in the early days of European civilization, been a most fertile source of legends of monsters and prodigies of all kinds. In mediæval times nearly every great city in Europe possessed one or more gigantic figures (constructed of wickerwork or light material of the kind), which were carried in procession on days of festival, and were supposed to represent tutelary deities or mythical personages. Legend grew up around these purely "decorative"

emblems ; Gog and Magog are still preserved in the
City of London, and the effigy of a similar giant is to be
seen in the museum at Salisbury.

But, apart from these incitements to develop legends
of giants, we have the finding in the ground of huge bones
and teeth—those of the mammoth or Arctic elephant—
which have been at different times and in various towns
of England and Europe believed to be the bones and
teeth of gigantic men. The giants in the arms of the
cities of Basle and of Lucerne apparently owe their
origin to the finding of such bones, and to the report of
the physician, Felix Plater, who examined some bones dug
up in the year 1577 in Switzerland, and declared them to
be those of a human giant 19 feet high. ·Such bones
were considered even in the last century as genuine
relics of the giant men who once inhabited the earth.
Bones of whales brought home by sailormen, as well as
those of fossil mammoths, still do duty in historic castles
for the remains of dragon-like monsters or gigantic men.

The mere exaggeration of one who tells the story of
the strange sights he has met with during his travels in
remote lands is responsible for a large part of the belief
in races of giants. The ancient Arabian voyagers
visited Madagascar, and saw the eggs and bones of the
big extinct bird, the Æpyornis, of which the museums of
London and Paris contain many specimens. Possibly
they may even have seen the living birds. The egg of the
Æpyornis is certainly big—much bigger than that of an
ostrich, about three times its length and breadth. But
such is the human habit of exaggeration that in the story
of Sindbad the Sailor, told in the wonderful " Thousand
Nights and the One Night," the egg has become as big
as the dome of a mosque, and the bird is represented as

easily carrying Sindbad into the Valley of Diamonds.
In the early Spanish accounts of Patagonia (Pigafetta's
" Voyage Round the World ") the inhabitants are
represented as being of such a monstrous size that the
heads of the Spanish sailors barely reached to their
waists ! This tradition of the gigantic size of the Pata-
gonians is still current. I was brought up on it myself.
In reality, they are merely a fine race, of an average height
of 5 ft. 11 in., identical with that of the inhabitants of
many districts in the north of Great Britain. It is probable that wherever early man, on his migrations, en-
countered and fought with a tall race he exaggerated the
size of his opponents and gradually magnified them to
the size of giants. Or, to put it more precisely, the man
who heard the first account and related it to a later generation added a bit to the stature of the big race, and that
generation, in relating the story to the next, added a little
more, and so on, as in the story of the three black crows.
That story, though no doubt familiar to most of my
readers, is too instructive—as an example of the manufacture of a legend by inaccurate repetition of hearsay
evidence—to be passed over when an opportunity occurs
for its quotation. Mr. X., a resident in a remote village,
is informed by a neighbour, Mrs. Smith, that a wonderful
thing has occurred in their midst—in fact, old Mrs.
Jones has vomited three black crows, which were no
sooner seen than they spread their wings and flew away.
Mrs. Smith states that she did not see the birds herself,
but was fully informed in regard to the occurrence by
that trustworthy party, Mrs. Brown. Mr. X. accordingly
calls on Mrs. Brown and asks for her version of the
occurrence. She declares that she had not stated that
three black crows were ejected by old Mrs. Jones, but only
one, and that she was assured of this by Mrs. Robinson,
who saw the bird. Accordingly Mr. X. hunts up Mrs.

Robinson and inquires of her as to this wonderful bird.
Mrs. Robinson is much astonished and annoyed. She
declares that what she said was that old Mrs. Jones had
vomited " something as black as a crow," and there Mr.
X. leaves the matter, satisfied with having traced a legend
to its actual basis of fact. Many marvellous legends,
popularly accepted as true, have originated in an equally
crude perversion of a statement of a not very unusual
occurrence, as it has passed from the original truthful
narrator through a series of wonder-loving storytellers.

The remains of extinct races of men which have
been dug up furnish no evidence of the former existence
of " giants," nor does any race of men larger than that
inhabiting the northern parts of Great Britain exist at the
present day. On the other hand, it is the fact that a
" pygmy race " of men is found in tropical Africa and
parts of Southern Asia. They range from about 4 feet
to about 4½ feet in height. Wild species of animals have
usually a definite size characteristic of the species, and
show but a small range of variation in measurement,
though sometimes a " local race," of larger or smaller size
than that which is usual, is observed. The puma (Felis
concolor) is one of the most variable in size among the
larger wild animals. Many reptiles and fish (as well as
many of the lower aquatic invertebrate animals) appear to
have no definite limit of growth, but to continue to increase in bulk as long as they live. Hence exceptionally
large individuals (*e.g.* of crocodiles, snakes, pike, lobsters,
whelks, and mussels) are occasionally found. But
among the warm-blooded vertebrates—the mammals and
birds—though very large species and very small species
of the same genus are not uncommon (such as the pygmy
hippopotamus of Liberia and the full-sized species of the
Nile and other African rivers, the large and small species

of true deer, of bovines, of cats, etc.), yet giants and dwarfs within the ranks of a single species, such as we know in the case of man, are not found except in domesticated races. Natural selection sternly eliminates all aberrations in size, whether giants or dwarfs.

CHAPTER XXIII

MORPHOLOGY AND MONSTERS

WHEN I was director of the Natural History Museum, I frequently received letters about four-legged chicks, double-headed lambs, and cyclopian (one-eyed) pigs, often accompanied by specimens. One I remember was addressed to " The Keeper of the Freaks, South Kensington," and having been, very naturally, delivered first of all at the neighbouring Art Museum (now the Victoria and Albert Museum) was passed on with something like indignant repudiation to me at the Natural History Museum. I was for some years kept in touch with " the freaks " by letters sent to the office of " The Daily Telegraph," and will therefore say a few words here about these curious natural productions.

In order that my readers may appreciate the interest and significance of these " monsters," it is necessary to give a brief sketch of a very difficult subject, which we may call the " Laws of Form," studied by zoologists and botanists under the name " Morphology," the name given to it by the great German Goethe who was poet, naturalist, and philosopher. I am all the more anxious to say a few words on this subject, since it is that which it has been my greatest pleasure, as well as my chief business to study and to teach, during the best part of my life.

If we look at the lifeless material of which the surface

and crust of the earth—as well as its interior—is composed, we find that n the absence of the hand of man and of the living bodies of plants and animals, the masses of material which project here and there on the general surface are very irregular, either angular or rounded, but not symmetrical (that is with opposite sides alike), nor capable of being grouped into various classes of like shapes. All, in fact, differ so much from one another, that we must conclude that their shapes are due, not to intrinsic laws or rules requiring certain known patterns of shape to be assumed by this rough material, but to the conflicting action of a number of external forces. Thus, we find water wearing down the hard material, excavating valleys, leaving irregular mountains and pinnacles, spreading flats of gravel and mud, with broken rock sometimes interspersed, over the valleys. We find wind blowing and piling up sand, and as " sand-blast " cutting and polishing here and there. We find earthquakes shattering the rocks and opening irregular chasms in the solid ground. We find the sea irregularly wearing away the land at one place and piling up " beach " at another, so as to give irregular outlines to our coasts. We see the glaciers of the mountain-sides grinding and polishing, and the ice as it forms splitting the rocks into irregular shapes. Clearly all these ceaseless changes are due to law-abiding necessary causes, but the result of their operation is not to produce any recognizable shapes of definite pattern, excepting so far as this is true of the vaguely tree-like shape of the furrows or cuttings, caused by the convergence of rivulets to form streams and streams to form rivers ; a shape which may be studied in the minute rivulets formed by the draining water on the sands uncovered by the sea at low tide.

Even when we come to look at the small bits of this

mineral surface of the earth we find as a rule that they
are irregular, of varied shapes and sizes, angular rock
fragments or water-worn rounded pebbles and grains of
endless variety and individual form. Soon, however, a
closer examination will reveal here and there more or
less abundantly in sands and gravels and rock fragments
those beautiful shapes which are called crystals, usually
of minute size, but sometimes an inch, or even a foot,
in length. " Crystals " are solid " geometrical " figures
bounded by flat surfaces and straight lines. They are
cubes, octahedra (eight-faced blocks), dodecahedra
(twelve-faced blocks), pyramids, six-sided, and four-
sided columns and needles, and other shapes. Some are
upright, like a cube or an oblong block with vertical
sides ; others have their sides set obliquely or slantwise ;
but all are extremely regular, sharply " cut," as it were,
and are classified into a perfectly definite limited series of
primary shapes or patterns, some of which I have just
mentioned. They are sometimes white and opaque,
sometimes coloured, sometimes transparent and colourless, sometimes beautifully tinted. Rock-crystal,
amethyst, common salt, selenite, iceland-spar, emerald,
topaz, garnet, diamond, fluor-spar, felspar, pyrites,
galena (lead ore) are a few examples of " crystals "
which are found in the crust of the earth. They have
been produced, some in the molten rocks of igneous
origin, some in sedimentary rocks deposited by water.
A most important fact is that they are " pure " chemical
compounds, not mixtures. A lump of mud is an impure
mixture of a great number of particles of many different
chemical compounds, which can be separated from one
another by rubbing the mud up in water, and letting the
particles separate and subside, whilst a gentle stream is
set up in the water, which carries some of the varied
particles farther than others.

A crystal (though sometimes it " includes " impurities and a large quantity of water, called " water of crystallization ") is either a pure " element," such as carbon, sulphur, copper, gold ; or it is a single chemical compound, such as chloride of sodium (common salt), or fluoride of calcium (fluor-spar), or sulphide of lead (galena), or some other of a vast series of possible compounds.

I must for a moment stop to say what we mean by " a chemical compound." Chemists have discovered, in the course of centuries of heating and dissolving, and otherwise " torturing " the substance of things, that they can extract from natural bodies about eighty substances —some abundant, some very rare—which, do what you will to them, cannot be broken up so as to yield constituent substances.[1] They are the ultimate irreducible constituents of matter on this earth, and are called " the elements " (a curious word, signifying in Roman times the letters of the alphabet, drawn each on a block of ivory, such as children use in order to learn to spell). All material things consist either of these elements in a pure state, or of substances formed by combinations of the elements, two or more, in definite and fixed numerical proportion, according to weight. These definite combinations are called " chemical compounds," or " combinations," and are broadly distinguished from mere

[1] I must qualify this statement by substituting " have not been " for " cannot be." The discoveries of the last twenty-five years as to Uranium, Thorium, Radium, and Helium, lead to the conclusion that whilst the " elements " do as a rule defeat all attempts to break them into constituent substances, yet some do " decompose " into constituent bodies, and that it is not improbable that such a breaking down of elements into constituent bodies may be found to take place in other instances; and thus our notions as to the nature of what we call " elements " may be greatly modified.

mixtures. In chemical combination the original properties of the combining elements disappear, and quite new properties are shown by the compound. Thus, eight pounds of the gas oxygen chemically combine with one pound of the gas hydrogen to form nine pounds of water—and in that proportion only. Twenty-three pounds of the soft, light metal sodium (which floats on water), combine with 35½ pounds (neither more nor less) of the pungent, poisonous, yellow-green gas chlorine—to form the clear cube-shaped crystals of common salt—a substance as different from its constituent elements as it is possible to imagine. Such are "chemical compounds"—unions of two or more elements in absolutely fixed proportions, resulting in the formation of bodies of distinct properties, differing completely in cohesion, in colour, transparency, hardness, and chemical activity from the elements thus combined, which, nevertheless, can by appropriate methods be extracted from the combination and restored to their original state !

Nearly every chemical compound has one shape of crystal which is its specific shape and has no obvious relation to the crystalline shape of its constituent elements. The ultimate particles of the chemical compound have this particular crystalline shape, and they may adhere to one another only in sufficient number to form very minute crystals, or in other circumstances they may keep on joining one another and so build up single crystals of the same shape but immensely bigger. Crystals are formed most frequently when a chemical body which was in solution in water (or in other liquid due to great heat) ceases to be "dissolved" owing to the "drying up" (escape as a vapour) of the water or the cessation of the great heat. Crystals are formed when, owing to these and other causes, the crystalline particles of a chemically pure substance become separated from surrounding matter. They attract and adhere to one another, and form either a mass of small crystals or a group of conjoined crystals or one big crystal. The shape of the crystals depends on the shape of the ultimate crystalline particles (so small as to be invisible), which fit to each other in series, side by side, all facing the same way. In common salt the ultimate crystalline particles are cubes. You can see by looking at the table salt in a salt-cellar with a lens that it consists of small cubic crystals. But the best way is to make a strong solution of the salt in water and to let it " evaporate." If you hasten the evaporation by heat you will get only small cubes, but if you let it go on for a few days without artificial heat and put some threads of cotton or wool into the brine for the crystals to stick to, you can get quite large cubes as big as a pea. Common alum, which is a combination of sulphur, oxygen, and the metals aluminium and potassium, crystallizes in double four-sided pyramids called octahedra (eight-faced). By allowing it to crystallize slowly from its solution in water very large individual crystals as big as a man's fist may be obtained. When quite pure they are colourless, but minute quantities of iron when present in the liquid give them a pale red tint, and pale green, purple and blue crystals may be formed owing to the presence of traces of chromium, manganese, or copper. It is by such impurities that crystalline gems acquire their colour, both diamond and sapphire or ruby being colourless when pure, but occurring also with blue, red, and green colour. Sulphur melted in a crucible crystallizes as delicate needles when allowed to cool. Crystals of endless varieties of chemical compounds occur in natural rocks, and even the red oxygen-carrying substance of our blood—a definite chemical compound of carbon, hydrogen, oxygen, nitrogen, and iron—can be

14

induced to crystallize in the form of four-faced pyramids and of plates and needles having a four-sided skewed or oblique outline (see page 54). Here, then, we discover in these natural products called " crystals " a law of form, an inherent symmetrical shaping of solid material, which invariably shows itself in certain chemical compounds. Each has a particular shape of which the angles can be measured, being characteristic of or essentially belonging to that chemical compound. The number of possible kinds of crystalline shapes is limited ; whilst there are many thousand different chemical combinations. Consequently many of the latter have very nearly or quite identical crystalline form.

What is the cause of this form ? The form is a " property " of the ultimate structural particles dependent on and varying with their chemical nature. We can only speak of it as " crystallization " or " crystal formation," and we really cannot get any further in the way of stating how or why it occurs. There are solid bodies, such as glass, glue, gum, and pitch, the particles of which do not arrange themselves as crystals. When we break them, or otherwise examine into their " structure," we find that it is equal throughout. They do not break into definite angular-shaped figures nor show regular planes of strain and structure pervading every minutest part of the mass. They are called " amorphous," that is, without inherent deeply seated shape or form in their substance. Their particles exhibit simple cohesion. Cohesion is the name given to what is called " a molecular force "—the " attraction " exhibited by the particles of a solid body for one another. Rigidity, hardness, brittleness, malleability, are names for variations in its intensity. It resembles that universal attraction called " gravitation " exhibited by larger masses of matter for one another—of which the fall of an apple to the earth and the " pull " of the stars and planets and moons on one another are examples. But " cohesion " i; not exhibited until two particles of the same nature are brought very close indeed to one another. Adhesion is the name used when particles of different nature, as, for instance, water and stone, are concerned. Two highly polished surfaces of glass (or of metal) will—because their smoothness enables them to come very close to one another—when placed one on the other, cohere. They become united as one piece. This attraction for particle to particle comes into play at very close quarters, and only at very close quarters. Crystallization is apparently a peculiar " ordering " or " regulation " of cohesion. Crystalline cohesion is an active definite interference with the operation of the " molecular force " of simple cohesion.

It is an important fact that some chemical substances (chemical " species," we may say) occur both in the amorphous and the crystalline state. Thus the chemical species silica—the combination of the gaseous element oxygen and the solid element " silicon "—occurs in the crystalline state, as rock crystal, quartz, and chalcedony, and it also occurs as " amorphous " silica, called opal, and devoid of all crystalline structure. The only difference in the composition of opal and quartz is the presence of a little more solidified water in the one than in the other. And the amorphous silica, or opal, may, under conditions which are not precisely known, suddenly change into crystalline silica. Another case is that of the flexible " amorphous " sulphur obtained by pouring melted sulphur into water. This viscous sulphur, without a trace of crystalline structure when first prepared, in the course of a few hours begins to change its state of cohesion and becomes a mass of minute delicate crystals.

The " laws " or " rules " of crystalline cohesion have been profoundly studied, and are minutely known, though the existence of this determining force, with all its variety and relation to chemical composition, remains an ultimate fact, which we have to accept simply as we do that of " gravitation " and that of the " chemical attraction " of the elements for one another, resulting in their combination as " chemical compounds."

Our knowledge of crystallization is a part of " morphology," the law of form. It seems strange that one should write of this subject—crystallization—as an introduction to the understanding of four-legged chicks. What has a rock-crystal to do with a misshapen bird ? The answer is that there is an inherent compelling regulation of, or interference with, simple cohesion in the substance of living things which can only be compared with that strange direction or domination of cohesion in crystals which is called " crystal formation." No one suggests that what has been called " organic polarity " —the inherent tendency of the substance of plants and animals to assume definite symmetrical and self-repeating form—is the *same* thing as the tendency to take on crystalline form and structure. But the existence of the latter and its study may help us in some degree to conceive of the mechanism at the root of the former. In any case, they are the two great examples of natural production of regular, complex, definitely ordered form by processes having their seat in the very substance exhibiting the form. These marvellous ordered forms are not simply and directly wrought by the gross external agency of ordinary pressure and blow, though they are, of course, bound up with and eventually due to the universal change and flow of surrounding material things and modes of motion.   They are both due in different degree to " molecular forces " inherent in the substance of which they consist.

CHAPTER XXIV

MORPHOLOGY AND MONSTERS (*continued*)

THE resemblances between the growth and the form-properties of a living thing and those of a crystal are in some important respects very striking. A minute crystal (such as one of common salt or of alum) placed in water, in which many chemical compounds are dissolved, as well as that compound of which it is itself built up, will attract the dissolved particles identical with its own and add them to itself, thus " growing " in bulk. It will neglect and reject the other dissolved particles. Thus, in a mixed solution of alum, common salt, and sugar, a crystal of alum will pick out by attraction the dissolved alum and leave the other substances in solution. Similarly the germ of some living things, or, to take a more simple example, a small bit cut off from some plants (a bit of the leaf of Begonia prolifera is the best instance) will, when placed in damp soil, attract to itself chemical substances dissolved in the moisture which contain the chemical elements required by it as " food," and will add them to its substance, and thus grow into a perfect plant of large size.

There is, however, an important difference between the attractive action of living substance and that of a crystal. The crystal can only attract the dissolved particles, which are identical in composition with its own substance. On the contrary, the living thing takes up substances as " food " which contain the chemical elements it requires, but in different combinations from that in which they exist in " protoplasm," or living substance. Protoplasm has the unique property of altering the chemical combinations of the elements present in the matter taken in as " food " and recombining them so as to construct the very elaborate chemical combinations which exist in living substances. This is a very remarkable power possessed by living substance, and broadly distinguishes the nutrition and growth of living things from the attraction exerted by crystals in consequence of which there is an addition to the crystal of a ready-made chemical substance identical with that of which the crystal consists.

Another point in which the growth of living things resembles that of crystals is that the growing mass has a definite symmetrical and often elaborate shape, to which its growth is, as it were, constrained or self-restricted. As a matter of fact, the " shaping " of most living things is, far and away, more elaborate than that of crystals, since the outside differs from the inside, and a variety of parts, internal as well as external, are produced as growth proceeds, whereas the crystal, though it differs from an " amorphous " substance in having crystalline " structure," yet exhibits the same uniform structure throughout its mass.

If a crystal be allowed to grow very quietly in a solution of the chemical substance of which it consists it will often attain large size, as, for instance, will an octahedron or double-pyramidal crystal of alum. But very slight agitation of the liquid or other mechanical disturbance will upset the balance and unity of the crystalline growth ; it will suddenly change its mode of growth, and grow as two crystals joined to one another instead of a single one. And this may go further, so that many crystals will start growing in one mass, instead of the growth proceeding and keeping the form of a single enlarging crystal. It is important to notice that when two or several " units " of form thus arise from the disturbance of the growth of a single crystal the new or secondary units are precisely of the same form and character as the single one would have been, but smaller. A mass is built up by " repetition " of similar units of form instead of by the increase of one original unit. The same thing occurs in the growth of living forms. Sometimes an original unit of form goes on increasing in bulk and remaining as the one individual unit which started to grow. But most frequently the growing unit, after some increase, divides incompletely, and we get several conjoined units of similar form building up the living thing, and each growing simultaneously. The simplest form-unit of living matter (protoplasm) is the minute more or less spherical structure called a " cell." Some microscopic plants and animals (Protozoa and Protophyta) consist of single cells, which when they divide do so completely, and separate from one another to lead an independent existence. But in by far the larger number of living things these primary or simplest units divide and remain (like a group of crystals) in contact, and form large " many-celled " masses visible to the naked eye, and in many cases attain vast sizes, such as the whale or the cedar tree.

Not only that, but the many-celled masses themselves also acquire definite and restricted symmetrical and characteristic shape. They are called secondary units, or units of the second order.   In animals these secondary units have essentially the form of a hollow sac, built up by two layers of " cells," with a mouth at one end.   Some animals consist when full grown of a single secondary unit of this kind.   Such are sea-anemones and single polyps, also some of the simpler worms and the molluscs (mussels and snails)   But just as the primary units, by division and repetition, give rise to the sac-like secondary units, so very often do the secondary units also give rise by growth to aggregations of secondary units instead of becoming larger and larger and retaining their single character.   These more complicated units are called units of the third order or " tertiary " aggregates, and they, too, have their own special restricted shape and characters.   They vary greatly in the degree to which the secondary units, of which they are built up, are either obvious and nearly separate, or are closely united and fused so as to be bound closely together to constitute an individual of the third order.   Many animals resembling sea-anemones, after growing to a certain size as a single unit, proceed to form a second, and many more, from the original base by which the creature is attached to a stone or rock.   Thus a whole group of anemone-like individuals connected at their base arises.   This is a " tertiary aggregate," or unit of the third order.   It is thus that corals consisting of thousands of united polyps, come into existence.   The composite assemblage thus formed often acquires a shape of its own, tree-like or hemispherical, or, as in the " sea-pens " and " sea-firs," takes the form of a plume or palm leaf with a supporting stem and regularly paired " leaflets," each consisting of many anemone-like polyps.

Among animals one of the commonest modes of aggregation of secondary units to form tertiary units, aggregates, or individuals, is that in which the secondary units appear as a chain or string, following one another. Animals thus " composed " are often called " segmented animals." Tape-worms are of this nature, and so are the jointed or segmented worms or annelids, like the earth-worm and many marine worms (see Chapter V). So also are the great series of annulated or jointed animals which we know as centipedes, arachnids, crustaceans (crabs, lobsters, and shrimps), and the six-legged and winged creatures, the insects. In these cases each joint is, in essential and profound characters of structure and form, like its fellows. Each ring or segment has its pair of legs, modified for biting, or walking, or swimming, but essentially repetitions of one another ; each has corresponding vessels, nerves, renal tubes, and muscles. The whole animal is an aggregate of secondary units. Instead of remaining one single long secondary unit, it has broken up in the process of growth into a series of more or less distinct identical units—repetitions of one another—which remain united in a longitudinal series, just as the material which might form a single big crystal may take the form of a row of united smaller crystals of the same shape.

The " Repetition of Parts " is one of the outcomes of this substitution of aggregates of smaller units for simple swelling or increase of size of a single unit. The con-stituent units of a higher aggregate have each the same parts and properties as every other, though more or less " masked " and " latent." This is a fact of great importance in the study of the forms assumed, and the organs developed, by segmented or chain-like animals.

But " repetition of parts " occurs in both animal and vegetable forms in other ways than this. If we break off a piece from a crystal of alum, and then place the crystal in a solution of alum—the broken part is repaired by growth—new particles of alum are attracted to the injured spot, and the proper form and symmetry of the crystal are restored. It is to this definite balance of a crystal around guiding lines of form, or " axes," that the term " polarity " is applied. We recognize as well as " crystalline polarity " what is called " organic polarity " —a property of fundamental importance in the production of the forms of animals and plants. Many living things, if a piece be cut off from them, do not merely " heal," but, like a crystal, reproduce the lost part. If a frog's leg (or that of a reptile, bird, or beast) be cut off the wound will heal, but the leg does not grow again. If, however, the leg of a newt (the common little salamander-like amphibian of our ponds) be cut off the leg grows again, complete in every respect. I had in the museum at University College, London, a specimen of a newt, prepared by the celebrated physiologist, Sharpey, in which the right fore-leg had been cut off four times, and each time had been perfectly reproduced. The successive amputated legs were preserved in alcohol, alongside the complete animal, with its last-grown leg in position. Just as in the mutilated crystal so here (as is seen also in many other animals and plants) new growth took place, and the new material laid down was " constrained," forced into the shape both outside and in (for all the skeleton and muscles are complete) proper to that position. The growth was " dominated " by the " polarity " of the complete organic shape from which it grew as a part.

" Organic polarity " is the inherent " balance " of organic form—for instance, of the right and left sides, the front and the hinder end, the upper and the lower surfaces,

and further of one organ or part by another which may
be distant from it, and it includes the repetition in series
of like parts.   All these form-determining qualities are
in higher animals and plants very numerous and very
complex.   Parts and structures are to a large extent so
" balanced " in regard to one another that the increase of
one is regularly, and by a law of growth, accompanied by
the increase of another and often remote part, or by its
decrease.   The parts are said to be " linked " or " cor-
related," and the word " correlation " expresses one of the
most important and far-reaching laws of form and the
growth of form as observed in animals and in plants—a
law to which the morphologists of the present day give
too little attention.

Whilst in crystals the form and correlation of parts
are determined, once for all, by the chemical nature of the
crystal, the polarities and correlations determining the
endless varieties of form of living things have been
gradually accumulated by variation (variation — the
universal redistribution of matter and force more in-
cessantly and largely evident in living matter than in most
solids) of these qualities in individuals, and the selection or
survival of the fittest—which have, age after age, transmitted their qualities in the substance of the germs or
buds which they have thrown off to form new generations.
In the course of countless ages these polarities and correlations, which ultimately are but varied molecular structure
carrying varied molecular attractions, have accumulated
variously in the different lines of descent to an in-
conceivable degree—so that the branching pedigree
of living things possesses in every diverging branch
special and differing " polarities of living substance."
In every group of branches starting from a common
stem there is a community in, or common possession of, an

immense heritage of selected and inherited " polarities."
Surrounding agencies, forces of tension and pressure, heat
and cold, can act on this marvellously endowed living
substance so as to destroy it, or to force it a little into this
shape or into that shape. But such agencies can do
little. The real determining ultimate cause of form is in
each case, in each living thing, the immense and special
heritage within its substance of polarities and correlations derived from millions of ancestors, each of whom
has contributed a fraction. There is profound truth in
the old writer's statement, " All flesh is not the same
flesh : but there is one flesh of men, another of beasts,
another of fishes, and another of birds."

Just as the splinter of a crystal reproduces the whole
crystal, just as the body of the newt separated from its
limb reproduces the limb in perfect shape—just as the
bit of a green leaf nurtured on moist earth will grow into
a complete plant of stem, roots, leaves, and flowers—so
the microscopic particles specially thrown off by living
things as reproductive germs, spores, or egg-cells, grow
to the perfect form, and, being but bits of the parent,
they inherit, as we say, or possess as a matter of course,
the properties and polarities of the parent of which
they are only little bits. They grow to full size, and with
wonderful precision the little shapeless mass, as it takes
in nutriment and grows, exhibits the " polarities," the
compelling form-scheme of its parent.

In a vertebrate animal, say a full-grown chick, the
right and left sides are alike ; they more or less exactly
balance or represent one another in structure. During
its growth in the egg the chick is a long streak with
similar right and left sides. The rudiment of a right
and of a left wing appear simultaneously, and the rudi-

ment of a right and a left leg. The streak takes form as a series of segments, repetitions of one another—following one another in line—the vertebral segments. The head and neck " balance " the tail ; the hind-limbs are in essential details of structure merely repetitions of the fore-limbs—the wings. This is more clearly seen in fishes, where the fore and the hind paired fins are but two fan-like concentrations or bunches of fin-rays which in ancestral fishes were spread along the whole length of the body—a single fin-ray to each vertebral segment. The wonder is not that these agreements and exact " shapings " sometimes go wrong during early growth from the germ and so form " monsters," but that they keep true to pattern in so many thousand individuals whilst only one is born in which some kind of failure occurs. The failures, or incomplete or redundant formations, die at a very early age in most animals. In fish-hatcheries, where tens of thousands of young fish are hatched out from their eggs in tanks under human care and easy observation, quite a large number of " monstrosities " make their appearance, but soon die, owing to their inability to compete with their brethren for food and safety, unless specially separated from them and reared with skill.

A common kind of monstrosity is the more or less complete division of the very young embryo into two, just as a growing crystal may divide into two conjoined crystals. This dividing process may affect the head only, so that you get two-headed monsters, common in very young fish, in chicks, and in lambs, and even in human embryos. Or, again, the division may affect only the hinder part, and thus you get everything else as usual excepting two complete pairs of hinder fins, or two complete pairs of hinder legs. The actual cause of the disturbance—of the failure in correct growth and the incomplete division into two—is not altogether clear, though experiments have been made on the eggs of fishes and fowls and " artificial " monsters have been thus produced. It is certain that the failure is due to mechanical or to physiological causes which have operated naturally at a very early stage, when the growth of the shapeless germ of highly sensitive form-determined protoplasm was but just commencing. We may now pass to a brief account of the chief forms of " monsters " produced by higher animals.

CHAPTER XXV

VARIOUS KINDS OF MONSTERS

TO one who has read the preceding chapter, it will not appear surprising that what are called "monsters" are born from all sorts of living things. They are usually offspring of unusual and astonishing shape, yet keeping within definite lines of symmetry and of likeness to the parents, differing grotesquely from the latter, yet agreeing with them in intimate structure. The polarity, the balance of parts shown in normal healthy individuals is obviously operative, but it fails, and, as it were, blunders in its work. Plants as well as animals exhibit such monstrosities. All "double" flowers are of this nature, the innate identity of the stamens and carpels with the leaf-like petals suddenly asserting itself by the appearance of stamens and carpels in the shape of petals. The "green rose" is another monster in which the parts of the flower assume the form and colour of foliage leaves, a proceeding which has a certain "lawfulness" about it, since the foliage leaves and the parts of the flower are in ancestral plants one and the same series of organs or parts. In Kew Gardens there is a rose-bush which produces these interesting green roses. The "fasciate" asparagus and coxcomb are monsters which are "orderly," but incorrect, growths. Here I shall confine further statements to the monsters produced by the higher vertebrate animals, including man.

The interest and superstition which in past ages were connected with the birth of " monsters " are a part of the general system of " omen-reading " and " augury " which mediæval Europe received from the Romans, among whom it attained to a growth and importance so dominating that it is difficult, at the present day, to form a conception of its preposterous pretensions. Mankind have from the earliest times desired to know the future, and to be warned beforehand of impending danger. The wish has been father to the thought, or rather to a whole series of preposterous, unreasonable thoughts. The Romans elaborated most carefully a plan of inspecting the entrails of animals (especially the liver) killed for the purpose, in order to obtain from their individual differences a pretended indication of lucky and unlucky action on the part of the individual for whom the inspection was made. A highly respected profession, well paid and handed on from father to son, existed, charged with the duty of reading the " will of the gods " in the signs sent by them in the entrails of dead animals, and also in the flight of birds (auspicium, avi-spicium, or bird-viewing). This profession persisted even into Christian times, and the picture of an early saint has lately been shown to represent him as carrying in his hand a pig's liver—the emblem of his profession as an augur—a curious object, the nature of which had long puzzled the learned.

It is not wonderful that we still find in country places a belief in divination and the omens given by birds. Probably a true and really effective study by primitive man of the movements of birds, guiding him as to the position of food or water or indicating certain changes of season, preceded the utterly foolish system of augury. It has constantly been the fate of man to create worthless

15

superstition from the truthful and valuable teaching of preceding generations.   There is, on the whole, a slight— but only a slight—general improvement in this matter among the educated classes of civilized communities. In the Far East for many ages the prosperous classes have accepted a system of divination (called geomancy) by reference to the shape of the land—hills, valleys, and rivers.   In the time of the Stuarts we, in England, were still willing to be directed by the elaborate imposture called astrology, and quite a large number of ill-educated women in the well-to-do classes (as well as their kitchen-maids) believe at the present day that their future can be foretold by the inspection by an expert of the folds of skin on the palms of their hands.   This method of augury was not practised by the Romans (who preferred a good solid liver for the gods to mark their will with), but it is of very ancient use in China.   The indications, however, recognized by the Chinese are quite contradictory of those admitted in recent European palmistry.   Both are baseless inventions.

The foregoing remarks are introductory to the statement that even such a man as Martin Luther was much troubled by the birth in his day of a monstrous calf (I do not know whether it was two-headed or eight-legged). He writes of it as pointing to some great impending event, and expresses the hope that the catastrophe may not be the last day itself.   A hundred years later, Evelyn, the cultivated country gentleman and courtier, and early Fellow of the Royal Society, does not hesitate to advance a similar belief in regard to another class of natural " monster."   He says : " The effects of that comet, 1618, are still working in the prodigious revolutions now beginning in Europe, especially in Germany."

In yet earlier times treatises concerning animal and human monsters were written, and they were regarded as of vast significance and importance. The chief kinds were named as follows : The Siren (having the form of a mermaid, the two legs being united or fused to form a sort of tail), the Janus (a two-headed monster), the Satyr (a human being with a distinct tail), the Cyclops (a monster with one eye in the centre of the forehead, instead of a pair). Others were enumerated, but in some cases actual animals newly brought from distant lands, and therefore unfamiliar, were confused with the exceptionally misshapen offspring of ordinary animals and of man. So little was known, so much was new and unfamiliar in those remote days, that any story of a monster was accepted as true. Now we have a fairly complete knowledge of the kinds of living things in all parts of the world, and can assign specimens to their proper groups and to regularly recurring causes.

Animal monsters of the vertebrate class are nowadays divided first of all into those which are due to simple mechanical injury and deformation and those which are due to a more subtle change, resulting in a modification of the natural growth with irregular or incorrect assertion of symmetry and polarity. The first group is very limited. The most usual case is that of the amputation during intra-uterine life of limbs or fingers or toes. Such deformations are not " paired " or regular, and are due to the accidental nipping or pressure on the amputated parts by displaced uterine membranes or cords during the foetal growth. The second group is the more curious and varied. These monsters may be classed as those due to (1) redundancy of growth ; (2) reversed position of the viscera (right placed as left and left as right) ; (3) defective closure of the growing embryo in the mid-line ; (4)

hermaphroditism ; (5) fusion of parts related by organic polarity to one another ; (6) double monsters (the most striking in appearance).

With regard to monsters showing redundancy of parts, cases are common both in animals and man of an extra finger or toe on all four limbs or on one pair, and specimens are to be seen in our chief museums. Domestic cats with six toes on each foot are not uncommon. A horse is sometimes born with three hoofs, or even four. Julius Cæsar is said to have had a favourite horse of this description. Extra vertebræ in the spinal column sometimes occur, also two rows of teeth instead of one. Long hair like that on the head sometimes occurs all over the face, so that a " parting " can be made from the tip of the nose to the back of the head. Nipples and mammary glands in excess of the pair proper to human beings sometimes occur irregularly scattered on the body, to the number of seven or eight, and a case is recorded where one of large size grew in the middle of the back. Supernumerary mammæ are commoner in men than in women. A second external ear sometimes occurs, and a second and third pair of holes like that protected by our ear-conch sometimes are found. This is the persistence of a second and third pair of gill-slits, which in vertebrates above fishes regularly close up in early embryonic life and disappear. The ear-hole or " external auditory passage " is really the first of the gill-slits, and does not disappear as the others do, though it is closed within by the delicate membrane called the " drum " of the ear.

The reversed position of the viscera is not very uncommon in man—the heart is on the right side and the liver on the left. Defective closure of the mid-line in embryonic growth leads to " spina bifida " and also to " hare-lip," but in extreme cases results in complete defect of the crown of the head and the production of a brainless monster which does not survive birth for more than a few days.

The condition known as " hermaphroditism," that is, the presence of the testis or sperm-producing organ and the ovary or egg-producing organ in the same individual, is the usual and regular thing in many lower animals ; for instance, in the little green polyp or Hydra, in a great many worms (including the earth-worm and river-worms), and in many snails, slugs, and clams. This was the earlier condition of animals, and distinct sexes have been produced subsequently by the suppression of either ovary or testes. Hermaphroditism does not occur in vertebrate animals as a regular and normal thing except in certain species of sea perch (Serranus), from the Mediterranean. In some other fishes (cod, herring, and flat-fish) as a rare exception a testis and an ovary are found in the same individual. And in toads and frogs minute aborted ovaries occur in the male, and small testes sometimes in the female. In all higher vertebrates true hermaphroditism is quite unknown. The female has no trace of testis, the male no trace of ovary. But in the mammals the external parts connected with these organs have an essentially identical plan of structure, and at an early period of foetal growth are indistinguishable. Cases occur in which the external organs of the adult male resemble (though differing clearly enough from) those of the female, and vice versa. These cases are often called " hermaphrodites," although they are really, in regard to the essential organ, either male or female, and are not true hermaphrodites at all. The fact of the existence of this monstrosity (cases of which are well known at the present day) gave rise to the Greek fable of " Hermaphroditus," and to the statues in Paris and Rome known by that name.

The fusion during growth of parts related by polarity leads to the uniting to one another of the fingers or of the toes, two or more ; also to the fusion of the legs, as in the monster called the Siren.   It is worth pointing out that no such fusion of the legs has occurred in the formation, either of the seals or the Dugongs and Manatees, nor in that of the whales, although such an explanation of their form has been sometimes suggested. The most curious case of a monster by fusion is known by the name " Cyclops," or one-eyed monster.   This occurs in domesticated animals, and is not rare in the pig.   The two orbits are fused in the middle line, and there is only one eyeball (sometimes there are two close together in one orbit).   The nose at the same time undergoes a change, forming a short trunk which projects from the forehead above the single eye.   The mouth is round and minute, or absent altogether.   These monsters do not survive more than a few days after birth.

Double monsters (to which group the four-legged chick belongs) are best traced from the most complete case of doubling, namely, complete separation of the two halves resulting from fission.   We can then arrange, as a series, the various phases of incomplete " doubling." Human twins are of two kinds, namely, identical twins and ordinary twins.   Ordinary twins are due to two " ova " or egg-cells being discharged from the ovary into the uterus at the same time, instead of a single one.   In many mammals a number of young are started in this way—what we call a " litter."   On the other hand, " identical twins " start from a single ovum, which on arriving in the uterus (we do not know precisely why) divides into two completely. Identical twins are always of the same sex (a very important fact when the question arises as to what determines the sex of offspring), and have a wonderful closeness of similarity in appearance and character. This multiplication by division of the very young embryo occurs in the Armadillos as a normal thing. Occasionally this rare tendency of the minute germ or egg-cell to divide into two does not fully assert itself, but results in an incomplete division of the ovum into two. The division is usually such as to pass along the middle line from back to front, and where it is incomplete we find two symmetrical individuals resulting, which are more or less completely joined side by side. In rarer cases the division of the ovum is such as to traverse the mid-line from right to left, and often results in two united individuals of very unequal size. Rarely such cases have survived to maturity, and one is known (and shown by a model in the museum of the College of Surgeons) in which a full-grown man had projecting from his chest the body and limbs of a small second individual not bigger than an infant.

The symmetrical right and left double-monsters are commoner. The celebrated Siamese twins were of this nature, being united by only a narrow band of flesh, extending from the lower part of the body. The division of the egg-cell was very nearly complete in their case. Other cases are known in which the head and arms and front part of the body of the two individuals are distinct, as also the two pairs of legs, but there is a union of the lower part of the two vertebral columns and of the pelves. This was the case with the " Two-headed Nightingale," Millie and Christina, and with other well-known examples. The former could sing in distinct parts by each head, and could use all four legs separately and rhythmically. Each head could control either or both pairs of legs ! In birds you may get the division both before and behind, so as to give two heads and four legs, or you may have the " splitting " limited to the hinder region, so as to give a normal one-headed bird with two pairs of legs. All degrees and varieties of this dividing along the middle line are found from time to time among the offspring of domestic animals and birds. A great field for the study of these monsters is furnished by fish-hatcheries, where large numbers of them are born and can be secured by the naturalist, though they rarely, if ever, grow to any size, their misshapen bodies preventing them from catching food and escaping from predatory enemies. I have examined a two-headed dogfish, which was captured in the sea and was 12 inches long.

The two-headed monster called a Janus is a doubled or split monster in which only the head is involved, and the splitting may be so slight that though there are two faces, there is only one brain-case and one brain. It is important to remember that none of these double monsters are due to a fusion of two originally distinct embryos. Always they are due to a very early division of the embryo into two, which may be of minimal extent or may be nearly or quite complete.

CHAPTER XXVI

TOBACCO

APART from the question as to whether the smoking of tobacco is injurious to the health or not, there are many curious questions which arise from time to time as to the history and use of tobacco. I have no doubt that for children the use of tobacco is injurious, and I am inclined to think that it is only free from objection in the case of strong, healthy men, and that even they should avoid any excess, and should only smoke after meals, and never late at night. The strongest man, who can tolerate a cigar or a pipe after breakfast, lunch, and dinner, may easily get into a condition of " nerves " when even one cigarette acts as a poison and causes an injurious slowing of the heart's action.

A curious mistake, almost universally made, is that of supposing that the oily juice which forms in a pipe when tobacco is " smoked " in it, or at the narrow end of a cigar when it is consumed by " smoking," is " nicotine," the chief nerve-poison of tobacco. As a matter of fact, this juice, though it contains injurious substances, contains little or no " nicotine." Nicotine is a colourless volatile liquid, which is vaporized and carried along with the smoke ; it is not deposited in the pipe or cigar-end except in very small quantity. It is the chief agent by which tobacco acts on the nervous system, and through that on the heart—the agent whose effects are sought and enjoyed by the lover of tobacco. A single drop of pure nicotine will kill a dog. Nicotine has no aroma, and has nothing to do with the flavour of tobacco, which is due to very minute quantities of special volatile bodies similar to those which give a scent to hay.

Most people are acquainted with the three ways of " taking tobacco "—that of taking its smoke into the mouth, and more or less into the lungs, that of chewing the prepared leaf, and that of snuffing up the powdered leaf into the nose, whence it ultimately passes to the stomach A fourth modification of the snuffing and chewing methods exists in what is called the " snuff stick " According to the novelist, Mrs. Hodgson Burnett, the country women in Kentucky use a short stick, like a brush, which they dip into a paperful of snuff ; they then rub the powder on to the gums. Snuff-taking has almost disappeared in " polite society " in this country within the past twenty years, but snuffing and chewing are still largely practised by those whose occupation renders it impossible or dangerous for them to carry a lighted pipe or cigar—such as sailors and fishermen and workers in many kinds of factories and engine-rooms.

One of the most curious questions in regard to the history of tobacco is that as to whether its use originated independently in Asia or was introduced there by Europeans. It is largely cultivated and used for smoking throughout the East from Turkey to China—including Persia and India on the way—and special varieties of tobacco, the Turkish, the Persian, and the Manilla are well known, and only produced in the East, whilst special forms of pipe, such as the " hukah " or " hooka," the

" hubble-bubble," and the small Chinese pipe are distinctively Oriental. Not only that, but the islanders of the Far East are inveterate smokers of tobacco, and some of them have pecul'ar methods of obtaining the smoke, as, for instance, certain North Australians who employ " a smoke-box " made of a joint of bamboo. Smoke is blown into this receptacle by a faithful spouse, who closes its opening with her hand and presents the boxful of smoke to her husband. He inhales the smoke and hands the bamboo joint back to his wife for refilling. The Asiatic peoples are great lovers of tobacco, and it is certain that in Java they had tobacco as early as 1601, and in India in 1605. The hookah (a pipe, with water-jar attached, through which the smoke is drawn in bubbles) was seen and described by a European traveller in 1614. Should we not, therefore, suppose that in Asia they had tobacco and practised smoking before it was introduced from America into the West of Europe ? It seems unlikely that Western nations have given this luxury to the East when practically everything else of the kind has come from the East to Europe—the grape and wine made from it, the orange, lemon, peach, fig, spices of all kinds, pepper and incense. Yet it is certain that the Orientals got the habit of smoking tobacco from us, and not we from them.

Incredible as it seems, the investigations of the Swiss botanist, De Candolle (see his delightful " History of Cultivated Plants "—a wonderful volume, published for 5s., in the International Scientific Series), and of Colonel Sir David Prain, formerly in India, and lately Director of Kew, have rendered it quite certain that the Orientals owe tobacco and the habit of smoking entirely to the Europeans, who brought it from America, as early as 1558. In the year 1560 Jean Nicot, the French Ambassador, saw the plant in Portugal, and sent seeds to France to Catherine de' Medici. It was named Nicotiana in his honour. But the introduction into Europe of the practice of smoking is chiefly due to the English. In 1586 Ralph Lane, the first Governor of Virginia, and Sir Francis Drake brought over the pipes of the North American Indians and the tobacco prepared by them. The English enthusiasm for tobacco-smoking, " drinking a pipe of tobacco," as it was at first called, was extraordinary both for its sudden development, its somewhat excessive character, and the violent antagonism which it aroused, and, as we learn from Mr. Frederic Harrison, still arouses. It was called " divine tobacco " by the poet Spenser, and " our holy herb nicotian " by William Lilly (the astrologer, not the schoolmaster), and not long afterwards denounced as a devilish poison by King James. The reason why the English had most to do with the introduction of smoking is that the inhabitants of South America did not smoke pipes, but chewed the tobacco, or took it as snuff, and less frequently smoked it as a cigar. From the Isthmus of Panama as far as Canada and California, on the other hand, the custom of smoking pipes was universal. Wonderful carved pipes of great variety were found in use by the natives of these regions, and were also dug up in very ancient burial grounds. Hence the English colonists of Virginia were the first to introduce pipe-smoking to Europe

The Portuguese had discovered the coasts of Brazil as early as 1500, and it is they who carried tobacco to their possessions and trading ports in the Far East—to India, Java, China, and Japan, so that in less than a hundred years it was well established in those countries. Probably it went about the same time from Spain and England to Turkey, and from there to Persia. The

Eastern peoples rapidly developed not only special new forms of pipe (the hookah) for the consumption of tobacco, but also within a few years special varieties of the plant itself. These were raised by cultivation, and have formerly been erroneously regarded as native Asiatic species of tobacco plant.

The definite proof of the fact that tobacco was in this way introduced from Western Europe to the Oriental nations is, first, that Asiatics have no word for it excepting a corruption of the original American name tabaco, tobacco, or tambuco : it is certain that it is not mentioned in Chinese writings nor represented in their pottery before the year 1680. In the next place, it appears that careful examination of old herbariums and of the records of early travellers who knew plants well and recorded all they saw, proves that no species of tobacco is a native of Asia. There are fifty species of tobacco, but all are American excepting the Nicotiana suaveolens, which is a native of the Australian continent, and the Nicotiana fragrans, which is a native of the Isle of Pines, near New Caledonia.

Forty-eight different species of tobacco (that is to say, of the genus Nicotiana) are found in America. Of these, Nicotiana tabacum is the only one which has been extensively cultivated. It has been found wild in the State of Ecuador, but was cultivated by the natives both of North and South America before the advent of Europeans. It seems probable that all the tobaccos grown in the Old World for smoking or snuffing are only cultivated varieties—often with very special qualities—of the N. tabacum, with the exception of the Shiraz tobacco plant, which, though called N. persica, is of Brazilian origin, and the N. rustica, of Linnæus, a native of

Mexico, which has a yellow flower, and yields a coarse kind of tobacco. This has been cultivated in South America and also in Asia Minor. But tobaccos so different as the Havana, the Maryland and Virginian, the incomparable Latakia, the Manilla, and the Roumelian or Turkish—all come from culture-varieties of the one great species, N. tabacum.

The treatment of tobacco-leaf to prepare it for use in smoking, snuffing, and chewing requires great skill and care, and is directed by the tradition and experience of centuries. As is the case with " hay," the dried tobacco-leaf undergoes a kind of fermentation, and, in fact, more than one such change. The cause of the fermentation is a micro-organism which multiplies in the dead leaf and causes chemical changes, just as the yeast organism grows in " wort " and changes it to " beer." It is said that the flavour and aroma of special tobaccos is due to special kinds of ferment, and that by introducing the Havana ferment or micro-organism to tobacco-leaves grown away from Cuba, you can give them much of the character of Havana tobacco ! A very valuable kind of tobacco is the Roumelian, from which the best Turkish cigarettes are made. It has a very delicate flavour, and very small quantities of an aromatic kind prepared from a distinct variety of tobacco plant grown near Ephesus and on the Black Sea (probably a cultivated variety of N. rustica) are judiciously blended with it. This blending, and the use of the very finest qualities of tobacco-leaf, are essential points in the production of the best Turkish cigarettes. The so-called " Egyptian " cigarettes are made from less valuable Turkish tobacco, with the addition of an excess of the aromatic kind. It is a mistake to suppose that opium or other matters are used to adulterate tobacco The only proceeding of the kind which occurs is the mixing of inferior, cheap, and coarse-flavoured tobaccos with better kinds. Water and also starch are used fraudulently to increase the weight of leaf-tobacco. But skilful " blending " is a legitimate and most important feature in the manufacture of cigars, cigarettes, and smoking mixtures.

The first " smoking " of tobacco seen by Europeans was that of the Caribs or Indians of San Domingo. They used a very curious sort of tubular pipe, shaped like the letter Y. The diverging arms were placed one up each nostril, and the end of the stem held in the smoke of burning tobacco-leaves, which was thus " sniffed up " into the nose. The North American Indians, on the other hand, had pipes very similar to those still in use. The natives of South America smoked the rolled leaf (cigars), chewed it, and took it as snuff.

It has been suggested that, in Asia, smoking of some kind of dried herbs may have been a habit before tobacco was introduced—since even Herodotus states that the Scythians were accustomed to inhale the smoke of burning weeds, and showed their enjoyment of it by howling like dogs ! But investigation does not support the view that anything corresponding to individual or personal " smoking " existed. " Bang " or " hashish " (the Indian hemp) was not " smoked," but swallowed as a kind of paste before the introduction of tobacco-smoking in the East—as we may gather from the stories of the " Arabian Nights "—although the practice of smoking hemp (which is the chief constituent of " bang ") and also of smoking the narcotic herb " henbane," has now been established. Opium was, and is, eaten in India, not " smoked." The " smoking " of opium is a Chinese invention of the eighteenth century.

The Oriental hookah suggests a history anterior to the use of tobacco, but nothing is known of it. The word signifies a cocoanut-shell, and is applied to the jar (sometimes actually a cocoanut) containing perfumed water, through which smoke from a pipe, fixed so as to dip into the water, is drawn by a long tube with mouthpiece. It seems possible that this apparatus was in use for inhaling perfume by means of bubbles of air drawn through rose-water or such liquids, before tobacco-smoking was introduced, and that the tobacco-pipe and the perfume-jar were then combined. But travellers before the year 1600 do not mention the existence of the hookah in Persia or in India, though as soon as tobacco came into use this apparatus is described by Floris, in 1614, and by Olearius, in 1633, and by all subsequent travellers.

The conclusion to which careful inquiry has led is that though various Asiatic races have appreciated the smoke of various herbs and enjoyed inhaling it from time immemorial, yet there was no definite " smoking " in earlier times. No pipes or rolled-up packets of dried leaves—to be placed in the mouth and sucked whilst slowly burning—were in use before the introduction of tobacco by Europeans, who brought the tobacco-plant from America and the mode of enjoying its smoke, and passed on its seeds to the peoples of Turkey, Persia, India, China, and Japan.

CHAPTER XXVII

CEREBRAL INHIBITION

THE best golf-player does not think, as he plays his stroke, of the hundred-and-one muscular contractions which, accurately co-ordinated, result in his making a fine drive or a perfect approach ; nor does the pianist examine the order of movement of his fingers. His " sub-liminal self," his " unconscious cerebration," attends to these details without his conscious intervention, and all the better for the absence of what the nerve-physiologists call " cerebral inhibition " —that is to say, the delay or arrest due to the sending round of the message or order to the muscles by way of the higher brain-centres, instead of letting it go directly from a lower centre without the intervention of the seats of attention and consciousness. The sneezing caused in most people by a pinch of ordinary snuff can be rendered impossible by " cerebral inhibition," set up by a wager with the snuff-taking victim that he will fail to sneeze in three minutes, however much snuff he may take. His attention to the mechanism of the anticipated sneeze, and his desire for it, inhibit the whole apparatus. So long as you can make him anxious to sneeze and fix his attention on the effort to do so, by a judicious exhortation at intervals, he will not succeed in sneezing. When the three minutes are up, and you both have ceased to be interested in the matter, he will probably sneeze unex-

pectedly and sharply.   I was set on to this train of thought
by a recent visit to an exhibition of photographs.

There were many very interesting illustrations of the
application of photography to scientific investigation.
Among others I saw a fine enlarged photograph of the
common millipede (Julus terrestris), and my desire was
renewed to have a bioscopic film-series of the movements
of this creature's legs.   Some years ago I attempted to
analyse, and published an account of, the regular
rhythmic movement of the legs of millipedes.   I found
that the " phases " of forward and backward swing are
presented in groups of twelve pairs of legs, each pair of
legs being in the same phase of movement as the twelfth
pair beyond it.   But instantaneous photography would
give complete certainty about the movement in this case,
and in the case of the even more beautiful " rippling "
movement of the legs of some of the marine worms.
Some kindly photographer might take up the investigation and prepare a series of films.   The problem is
raised and the effects of " cerebral inhibition " are described in a fanciful little poem written, I believe, by
a lady.   As it is not widely known, I give it here as a
record of " cerebral inhibition " :

> " A centipede was happy 'til
>   One day a toad in fun
>   Said, ' Pray, which leg moves after which ? '
>   This raised her doubts to such a pitch
>   She fell exhausted in the ditch,
>   Not knowing how to run."

The point, of course, is that she could execute the
complex movement of her legs well enough until her
brain was set to work and her conscious attention given
to the matter.   Then " cerebral inhibition " took place
and she broke down.

INDEX